I0117407

Joseph C. Sibley

Speech of Hon. Joseph C. Sibley, of Pennsylvania, in the House of Repreesentatives

Joseph C. Sibley

Speech of Hon. Joseph C. Sibley, of Pennsylvania, in the House of Repreesentatives

ISBN/EAN: 9783337422684

Printed in Europe, USA, Canada, Australia, Japan

Cover: Foto ©Suzi / pixelio.de

More available books at **www.hansebooks.com**

If you have whispered truth, do it no longer,
But speak as the trumpet does, louder and stronger.

SPEECH

OF

HON. JOSEPH C. SIBLEY,

OF PENNSYLVANIA,

IN THE

HOUSE OF REPRESENTATIVES,

FRIDAY, AUGUST 18, 1893.

SPEECH

OF

HON. JOSEPH C. SIBLEY,

OF PENNSYLVANIA,

IN THE HOUSE OF REPRESENTATIVES,

Friday, August 18, 1893.

The House having under consideration the bill (H. R. 1) to repeal a part of an act, approved July 14, 1890, entitled "An act directing the purchase of silver bullion and the issue of Treasury notes thereon, and for other purposes"—

Mr. SIBLEY said:

Mr. SPEAKER: In common with those who favor bimetallism, I had hoped that, before the consideration of this question should ensue, there would be offered some measure providing for the immediate relief of the business interests of this nation. We have heard from all the speakers that the nation is in a state of panic, and that industry is paralyzed from one commercial center to another can no longer be denied.

I came to Washington before the meeting of this body, in the sincere hope that some financial measure might be provided which should afford adequate relief. Many had been submitted to me by others. I had some peculiar ideas of my own. I found, however, that the distinguished gentleman from Ohio [Mr. JOHNSON] had prepared a measure which seemed to cover the entire ground; a measure which, if acted upon by this body, would set in motion all the industries of this country, and cause every spindle to hum throughout the length and breadth of this great land within ten days of its enactment.

By the passage of that bill we could have provided relief to the amount of $200,000,000 if necessary. I think I am speaking for all the friends of bimetallism when I say we can not be charged with being obstructionists to the business interests of this nation. The welfare of its citizens are as dear to us as to those gentlemen upon the other side. We were ready for the immediate consideration of a proposition which provided in simple and plain terms that the holders of United States bonds might deposit such securities with the Government, in its Treasury or subtreasuries or Governmental depositories, and receive therefor Treasury notes; the interest on the bonds ceasing during the time the notes were in circulation, the Government saving the interest, and the citizens, the business men, being provided with an abundant capital to carry on the industrial enterprises of the United States. Not a dissenting voice against the measure, or against any proper measure of relief, has been offered by those who stand here to-day as the champions of the people in this cause of bimetallism.

I received, and I presume every member of the House has received, a circular sent out from New York. It is a wonderful fact that all our financial wisdom and intelligence has to come from east of the Delaware River. That circular suggests legislation which provides that different classes of securities may be deposited with the Treasury, and when the great clearing houses of New York, Chicago, St.

Louis, New Orleans, and some of the other centers, decide that the country is in a state of panic, then the Government is to put up the money on their securities. Gentlemen, in my judgment the time has come in this nation when the clearing houses of these great cities shall no longer dominate and control the financial policy for sixty-seven million producers in this land. Their control has effected enough woe, enough disturbance, and has caused the shedding of sufficient tears.

Mr. Speaker, if the gentlemen on the other side accept the proposition of the gentleman from Ohio [Mr. JOHNSON], my speech ends right here. We will come together, not as partisans, but as patriots, and will decide this question of relief at this very moment, and relieve more than three million workingmen. You have told us about the trouble of capital; but there are three million of God's American citizens to-day who are vainly waiting for the opportunity to secure bread for their hungry ones. Winter comes on apace, and you will be held responsible for whatever consequences may occur, and not ourselves, for we stand on the pledge made in favor of bimetallism, in favor of the money of the people, against your determined opposition.

Mr. Speaker, it may be well for us to come right down to some of the causes of this panic. They have been hinted at, but it is about time we had them as they are. It is stated upon what seems to be the highest authority, before the close of the last Administration, there were prepared in the Bureau of Printing and Engraving $100,000,000 of 4½ per cent bonds, to be sold to the bankers of New York—at what price? At par. And upon what necessity? The necessity of maintaining the gold reserve at $100,000,000. Everybody well knows that the next day after these bonds had been issued and absorbed by these banks in exchange for their gold, they would have commanded a premium of 14, 15, or 16, thus providing a rake off that these people wanted to relieve you of. The stake was a big one. They had $15,000,000 represented on the board.

I tell you, gentlemen, that this is a big pile to have in front of men with the average greed and cupidity of the American citizen, assisted by some who are not American citizens. The Administration of Mr. Harrison refused that issue. Mr. Harrison is represented as having said that he wished his Administration to be known as one in which the debt had been reduced rather than increased; and when the new Administration came into power they found a diminished reserve, a reserve below what was called the legal limit of reserve.

Now, my friends, I do not know much about judicial law, but I do know something about the laws of business. In the conduct of my business I maintain a reserve. I consider that the only safe way for me to conduct my enterprises is to maintain a reserve fund in the bank, but when, in the exigencies of business, my deposit account is reduced down to the limit of that reserve, what do I do? Go and issue a mortgage upon my possessions? No, sir. I use the reserve fund that I have placed in the bank for that very purpose, rather than encumber my possessions with a mortgage. Why should not the Government do the same thing? The Secretary of the Treasury wisely "called" their "bluff." He held a "full hand" and they had a "bobtail." [Laughter.]

Further, we commenced to export gold; we exported it in payment of the balance of trade against us. We exported that gold and it went abroad, in part to pay the expenses of the 24,000 men of this nation who to-day own the half of our total wealth. They lived in sumptuousness and riotousness abroad, and our gold went there in part to pay their expenses. Then there were shipped from New York nearly five millions of gold each week. Any gentleman can take his pencil and paper and figure up that, at the rates of exchange prevailing at that time, each shipment of a million involved a loss of $2,000.

We sent out that gold; but who sent it? Were they American citizens? I do not know; they may have become so; but I know it was sent out by Heidelbach, Ickelheimer & Co. and by Lazarus, Frères & Co. They were the agents of the Rothschilds, who were exporting this gold. It was needed to refund the Austrian debt and place that country upon a gold basis. These men paid their premium of $2,000 on each $1,000,000 of gold, and then proceeded to get even. How did they do it? They went into the stock market and sold that market one hundred thousand shares short and gained a million. The depreciation of the values of securities traded upon in the city of New York since this "bear" campaign began has amounted to over $1,000,000,000.

Do you fear that gold is not going to come back into this country? I never had a doubt about it. They exported gold in pursuance of their unholy design to transfer the wealth of a continent into the coffers of a few English bankers located in Lombard street.

Let me show you, Mr. Speaker, if possible, how this thing has worked, and how it is working. All over the Continent of Europe the Rothschilds have their agencies. There is not a European capital or town where you do not find a branch of that house, and I take it that if matters go on as they have been going heretofore it will not be long until you can not find a city or a town in this country where the Rothschilds will not have a branch house.

They have drawn off our gold, and securities have depreciated 50, 60, even 90, per cent in value. Dividend-paying stocks have depreciated, and these gentlemen own them to-day, and have them locked up in their coffers.

Do you not think, then, that they are going to let gold flow back? I hold in my hand a copy of the New York World, which, I fear, comes nearer to being the revelation of the Lord Almighty to some of you than any other document that has been before your vision for the last few years. [Laughter.] This paper contains a cartoon which is entitled, "Wall street waiting for the lamb's wool to grow again." No one can claim that the New York World is a bimetallic paper. It is for a "sound and honest" money. [Laughter.] They are sound, honest men that own and control this paper; they were "born so." [Laughter.] This cartoon represents a distinguished lot of individuals, with their names, and their buttonhole bouquets, "waiting for the lamb's wool to grow again." Here is the stock exchange, where the poor lamb is standing, while the line of shearers reaches from the stock exchange away up as far as Trinity Church. See the length of their shears! Here is the poor lamb, every particle of his wool shorn from him, and they have even gashed into his hide, so that the blood is streaming from him! Of course they have got to wait for the lamb's wool to grow again! [Laughter.]

Why, Mr. Speaker, I raise Angora goats up in Pennsylvania, and I shear them only once a year. I find it more profitable to wait for a second crop. I cut my grass early in the summer, and I do not keep running the mowing machine over it every few days; but I wait until the fall for the aftermath. So these people will wait. There is no fear about the return of gold. They have got our securities, they have got mortgages upon our possessions, and now what do they want? Why, they want to see the wheels of industry revolve and to hear the spindles hum again, so that they may grow a new crop of wool, and then repeat the shearing process.

I see that my New York friends insist that there is but one remedy for this trouble, and that is the issue of bonds to maintain gold and put us upon a "solid financial basis." Well, gentlemen, suppose we agree to issue the $150,000,000 of bonds that you demand, how long will it be before you will want another $150,000,000? If through your conspiracy you can get this $150,000,000 that you say is necessary now, why can not you, three months hence, present your Treasury notes, your legal-tender notes, to the subtreasury and draw out the gold reserve again, and then come here and demand $150,000,000 more of bonds as an additional mortgage on the industries of the nation? An so, indefinitely, you can carry on this process until the wealth of an entire nation will not suffice to feed the greed of these conspirators.

You ask the cause of the panic. I do not know all the causes; but I know this: for two years the distinguished gentleman from Ohio [Mr. HARTER] has been a missionary in the field. The distinguished ex-member of the House, St. George Fred Williams, of Massachusetts, and the other saint from Ohio, have filled the columns of the Arena, the Forum, the North American Review, the American Journal of Politics, and other papers with their predictions of disaster to come if we did not get upon a solid gold basis.

The news and editorial columns of the metropolitan papers have contained the paid advertisements of the gold clique. The country weeklies have been sent tons of "boiler plates," accompanied by courteous and wily letters, asking the editors to use the matter as news, "for the good of the country;" and if they refused they were allowed to publish it at advertising rates. I do not blame the papers. They needed the money in these hard times. I only blame them for not marking their editorials and news "1 t., head of column, next to reading matter."

The gold-standard men have howled calamity for two years incessantly. And when a member of this House or a citizen of this nation predicted that this attack upon silver, this decrying of the credit of the nation, this lessening of the value of all products, could but bring disaster, you charged us with being calamity howlers. Yet if there has been more calamity howled than has been howled by our distinguished friends of the other side, I do not know where in the pages of literature to find it.

There have been other causes for this panic. They have been numerous. It has not arisen from any one cause. But I will tell you what in my humble judgment is one thing that was responsible for a portion of it. They have a club over in the city of New York called the Reform Club. I think the Speaker knows something about the Reform Club. [Laughter.] And that club undertook in advance of the assembling of this body to fix up and issue to the world what they called a "tariff" for our adoption.

Why, sir, they make our responsibilities easy and our labors light. But the people of this nation have said that they never elected those men to frame a tariff, that they elected us to deal with that question upon business principles, and with exact justice and honesty to all concerned. They have got a little afraid of your Reform Club over in New York, that assumes, sometimes even with the appearance of authority, to be responsible for the whole conduct of governmental affairs. The members of that club have attempted to name members of committees of this House; they have attempted to tell us what shall be our action on this financial question.

Another reason for your panic has been chargeable directly to the action of your Wall street gamblers, who have circulated rumors by the wholesale. They permitted one of these gamblers to go into their chamber a few weeks ago and announce that one of the greatest banks in New York had failed. And how did that body punish him for putting in circulation this false report? They suspended him for a year; and it is said his profits through bear operations since this panic commenced have netted him in clear cash over $10,000,000. I think he can afford to stand the suspension.

Another thing, my friends, that is responsible for this panic is your own New York bankers. You may stand here, the whole body of you, from that State, and talk about your patriotism and how you will uphold the business interests of the nation. But he who has eyes and has read current events knows better than that. When the Government refused to issue bonds, and when the banks of California, the banks of Chicago, and the great West came to the relief of the Administration by giving it gold, your bankers in published interviews, which are extant to-day in the columns of the New York papers, threatened to give the South and the West a pinch of hard times. I can show you those threats in your metropolitan papers. Your bankers threatened to give the people of the South and West a taste of hard times.

This conspiracy, which has had twenty years for its hatching, has now reached its culmination; and those who have taken part in it believe the time is now ripe for the consummation of these villainies and the wholesale robbery of the people.

Another thing, Mr. Speaker, which I think is responsible is the character and business pursuits of those who demanded this Congress be called in extraordinary session, or induced the Executive of this nation to call it. What genuine business interest in this nation asked for the assembling of Congress at this time? But the New York bankers and stock gamblers, in their interviews in the columns of their papers, day after day, said, "Let the call for an early session be issued, and at once the panic will stop and the country will be all right; business will find its ordinary channels; prosperity will dawn on every home." Was not that your prophecy? And from the day that the proclamation was issued down to this time we know that the financial situation has been getting worse.

Who made the demand for this extra session? Your boards of trade, your stock exchanges, your wreckers upon the shores of commerce, your gamblers, your vampires upon human industry. [Applause.] No body of agriculturists in this nation asked for a special session of Congress. No body of laboring men demanded that Congress should assemble. No, sir; the demand came not from the producers of a nation's wealth, but from the absorbers of a nation's wealth. [Applause.] This demand came not from the 67,000,000 of American citizens, but from the 24,000 who, through this financial villainy, have taken one-half of your total wealth, and now want to gain as quickly as they can the balance of it. [Applause.]

Mr. Speaker, I have heard much about the evils of a high protective tariff. I realize the force of what is said in that direction. But where tariff Saul has slain his thousands this financial David has slain his tens of thousands, and mutilated, maimed, and crippled his tens of millions. [Applause.]

Another reason for financial distrust and doubt is the fear of the people that the designs of those who have determined to destroy one-half of the metallic base of commercial transactions may prove successful. Bankers want bonds. Why, my friends, here is a proposition which I make to you bankers in this House and the 240 lawyers who are members of this body. I wish you would get together and illustrate to us how it is that a bond which rests only on the faith of the Government is good, is desirable, is wanted, is howled for, is conspired for; and yet a greenback, a Treasury note, which rests upon the same faith of the people in this Government, you denounce as "fiat money." I want to understand where and how you make your distinction.

Mr. LANE. The interest is the distinction.

Mr. SIBLEY. Yes, as my friend from Illinois [Mr. LANE] suggests, one carries interest and the other does not; one goes to a premium and the other maintains its parity.

My friends, it has been amusing to sit in this House and hear the diagnosis that the different schools of physicians and empirics have given of the malady of the patient. And they have got as many different maladies as there are different schools of doctors for their treatment. Here comes one who says the patient is sick, and the trouble with him is that there is lack of confidence. All he needs is to have confidence and he will soon be well again. Why, up in Pennsylvania the other day a bank closed its doors where I had several thousands of dollars on deposit.

Now, I have absolute confidence in the president of that bank; the people of that community have confidence in him, and he has confidence in me; but neither of us has any money. That is what is the trouble. [Laughter and applause.] I want to tell any man who proposes to heal this disease by administering a dose of confidence medicine that he has got to inject that medicine into every patient at the same time, everywhere in the country, or it will not work. You can not give a dose to a man in this community and another to a man in another community, and hope that your confidence medicine is going to cure.

But another says the difficulty arises from overproduction—overproduction of wheat, of wool, of oil, of coal, of corn, of cotton, and beef. Overproduction of cotton! Why, I drove out through the slums of Chicago four weeks ago and saw men, women, and children in tatters. Overproduction of wheat, and we read that in the West people are starving for the very necessities of life. Overproduction of fuel, and yet they froze to death in Pennsylvania, the land of fuel, last year. Overproduction of oil, and a million of our people roam in darkness this night for want of it. No, sir, it is not because of overproduction. It is because of under-consumption, because of the lack of the necessary money to purchase these absolute necessities of human existence. [Applause.]

But there are other classes of doctors, other schools, who tell us that we are getting down to "hardpan," that we have been going through an era of inflation, and that it is necessary for us to get down to first principles; and they say we are going down to hardpan. Why, my friend, the farmers, the workingmen of this country, were down to hardpan fifteen years ago. [Applause.] They got down to bed rock ten years ago. They went down to where they scorched the soles of their shoes five years ago, and they are getting to-day, in this year of our Lord 1893, down to the point where it is scorching their feet and the fumes and odors of hell come up to meet them. [Applause.] And yet we are told we are getting down to hardpan. I want to know how much further towards sheol we have got to go before we get there? [Laughter and applause.]

Mr. Speaker, I have been told, with others, that I must support this measure because it is a Democratic measure. When did the new prophet of the Lord arise, and when did he receive the last revelation of the Democracy? [Applause.] Certainly it must have been since the last national platform adopted by the Democratic party at Chicago. [Renewed applause.] My friends, you can not turn to a platform, with one exception, from the consummation of the crime of 1873 down to the present era that does not denounce that crime, that does not designate the men as criminals who perpetrated it, and that one exception is the old Bay State. Every State and every national platform has stood upon that principle, has declared this to be its judgment, this to be its pledge, that this crime against the laboring people, this crime against their happiness, should no longer go unpunished.

I may not understand Democracy, Mr. Speaker. I stand for the Democracy which has regard to the interests of the great masses as well as to those of the privileged few. I revere that Democracy which was taught by the fathers of the Republic, the Democracy of Jefferson, who stood for the rights of the people as against the aristocratic tendencies of New York and New England, which existed in those early days. New York and New England denounced him as a socialist, as a communist, and as a demagogue. He is what I call one of the fathers of the Democracy. Thomas Jefferson once wrote: "I can scarcely withhold myself from joining in the wish of Silas Deane that an ocean of fire rolled between the old world and this." Why, how that utterance would make some of our modern anglomaniac statesmen jump.

I stand by the Democracy of Andrew Jackson; and, my friends from New York and New England, Democrats and Republicans, what did you say of Andrew Jackson? He denounced your national banks and your stock exchanges, and said they were leeches and vampires upon the body politic. [Applause.]

What, I ask, did New York and New England say of Andrew Jackson in those days? They assailed him with every vile epithet that could be found and applied in the English language. Demagogue was your pet name for him. Why, your Democracy of New York made medals portraying Andrew Jackson sitting down behind a rail fence with the epaulettes on his shoulders, smoking his old corncob pipe, and his head surmounted by asses' ears. These medals are still extant, and you Democrats of New York issued them. And you people of New England, with your boasted seats of learning—your Harvard College conferred the degree of LL. D. on Andrew Jackson and then passed resolutions regretting such action. [Applause.]

Mr. Speaker, I stand by the Democracy of the old fathers of the Republic. I stand by the men whose voices have been raised always for human liberty; a Democracy that has regard to the cries of the suffering that have been heard in this land in all of its decades and history. I have regard for a Democracy that has respect to the man who toils, as well as the man who absorbs. I have respect for the Democracy that considers the right of the workers in the busy hive of industry, as well as of the drones who bask on the sunny side thereof.

Mr. Speaker, I stand by Democracy as exemplified by the first great Democrat who ever walked the face of God's fair earth; who said that he who was naked and hungry and sick was my brother; and that when we ministered to such an one we ministered to the very Christ; a Democracy which said that he who had fallen among thieves and was grievously wounded was my neighbor. And yet they crucified and put to death that first Democrat of the ages. My friends, did you ever think why they crucified the Lord Jesus Christ? They never crucified him because of any religious ideas that He possessed different from the masses. Babylon and Nineveh, Rome and Greece, had erected their altars of Pagan worship under the very eyes of the people without a protest; but they crucified that man because He said, "Woe unto you, Scribes and Pharisees, hypocrites." [Applause.] They crucified Him because He had condemned the extortioner and the oppressor, and had dared to scourge the money-changers from the temple of the living God. [Applause.] And whoever boldly stands to-day in the cause of humanity against the greed and rapacity of the few is a marked victim for crucifixion.

I have been asked repeatedly, since I came to Washington, how it occurred that I, a man of some reputed means, and hailing from Pennsylvania, could ally myself with the disordered ideas of bimetallists? Why, my friends, they still print and read Bibles up in the State of Pennsylvania. [Applause.] And on the page of that good old book the command is just as plain as it was the day it was thundered from Sinai, "Thou shalt not steal!" [Applause and laughter.] Why, my friends, if a man from Pennsylvania shall not stand for bimetallism, from what land shall the man hail to stand for it? William Penn came to Pennsylvania and he dealt justly and honestly with the poor red man; and he still has his followers in that blessed Keystone State who are willing to deal honestly and justly with the poor white man. [Applause.] Pennsylvania is rich in treasures of coal and iron, of oil and wheat, but she is richer still in her millions of sons and daughters who "know the right, and, knowing, dare maintain." [Applause.]

My friends, you tell us that we can not win this fight. Gentlemen get up here and cite the fact that England is against us, that Germany is against us, that Spain is against us, that France is against us, and they even come to me and tell me that the Administration is against us. [Laughter.] But I tell you, you may league all your forces, but you can not destroy the sparks of liberty on this continent. [Applause.] Switzerland has stood for years, a little gem surrounded by the crowned thrones and monarchies of Europe, and maintained her liberty. But you tell us the odds are against us. Well:

> Granted the odds are against us, granted we enter the field,
> When fate has fought and conquered, broken the sword and shield,
> When then? shall we ask for quarter, or say our work is done?
> Say, rather, a greater glory is ours, if the field be won.
> It is war with the wrong of years, with prejudice, pride, and hate,
> Against the world's decrees and the frown of an evil fate.
> A crown to the one who wins, and the worst is only a grave;
> And somewhere, somewhere still, a reward awaits the brave.
> A broken shield without, but a hero's heart within,
> And grasped with the hand of steel the broken blade may win.

[Applause.]

Why, Mr. Speaker, gentlemen tell us that all our arguments are as rot. I quote their exact language. They meet our arguments with subtle sophistries. They hurl walking encyclopedias, loaded to the muzzle, at us, and they justify their conduct upon any pretext or pretense they please. I remember when a boy reading in Æsop the fable of the Wolf and the Lamb. A wolf met a lamb, and was determined to devour it; but wishing to justify himself even in the sight of the lamb, held converse thus with him:

"Sir, last year you insulted me."
"No," meekly bleated the lamb, "last year I was not born."
"But you eat the grass out of my pasture."
"O, no; so far I have never tasted grass."
"But you drink at my spring."
"No; so far my mother's milk has been both food and drink to me."
Whereupon the wolf seized him and ate him, saying, "My fine fellow, in spite of all your argument you shall not rob me of my dinner."

[Laughter.]

The moral of the tale is that tyrants never lack pleas to justify their crimes.

But you call us cranks. I have heard that term applied to almost every man who in twenty years has stood out in advance of the common horde. Any man who stands in advance of the present is called a crank. They did not then have the name invented, but I fancy Columbus, Luther, Gallileo, Garrison, Lowell, Patrick Henry, and the great men who have made lasting impressions on the pages of the past were all denominated cranks or the equivalent term therefor.

You say that we are weak and obscure, and a lot of fanatics from the West that come from the farms, "and what can such men know about finance?" Why, my friends, I do not know but what these men, while they have been turning the furrow, have had as good opportunities as other people to turn over in their minds these great living problems which so closely affect their own well-being. The mechanic has stood at the lathe, and as the shaft revolved has also revolved in his own mind these problems; and I can not for the life of me understand why he can not attain as perfect an apprehension of them as the man who walks into the stock exchange at 10 o'clock in the morning and stays there till 3 o'clock in the afternoon, goes to his office and balances up his accounts, saunters up-town for a dinner at Delmonico's, goes to the theater, takes a box for the evening, and then sits in with the boys and plays draw poker until 4 o'clock the next morning. [Laughter.]

The very best business men, my friends, you have known in your lives came from the farm, and the only argument that I have seen that all those remaining on it were fools was from those who had not remained. [Laughter.] Oh, you say that they are a lot of obscure cranks back in the country. Why, your great New England poet, the champion and herald of human liberty, once said:

> Oh, Truth! Oh, Freedom! How are ye still born
> In the rude stable, in the manger nursed;
> What humble hands unbar those gates of morn,
> Through which the splendor of the new day bursts.

[Applause.]

My friends, I am not going to shoot much longer into the air, but going to come down to something practical.

I want to say a word, first, about the Administration. Men are told, and men have told me, that I have got to be very careful; that my political future was at stake; that they had grand schemes laid out for me for the future; and I had better be very cautious, or assume, at least, a very conservative attitude upon this great question. My friends, I have not got a particle of principle that is not too dear for me to trade for all the patronage that could ever be given out at the White House. [Loud applause.] And that office has never yet been created for which I will barter away any portion of that moral sense of obligation which I owe to my fellow-man and my God. [Renewed applause.]

I have too much respect, I have too much confidence in the honor and the integrity of the man who occupies that house to believe that such things are true. I believe that when he comes to me for an honest expression of opinion concerning the merits of any man, that he would rather take the opinion of one who has stood up boldly and told the truth, as it is given him to know the truth, than to take the opinion of a milk-and-water, namby-pamby man, who is always willing to

> Crook the pregnant hinges of the knee
> Where thrift may follow fawning.

[Loud applause.]

President Cleveland is an honest man from the ground up; he has the courage of his convictions, and I believe he has sincere respect for others who exercise such convictions. [Prolonged applause.]

Mr. Speaker, we have read of wreckers who, in olden days, giving false lights along the dangerous coast, would lure a stately ship, freighted with a valued cargo, upon the sunken rocks, that in the death and ruin they had by their false signals created they might revel in the spoils and plunder of wreck and ruin. And so we see to-day the grand old Ship of State freighted with the hopes and happiness of sixty-seven millions of human souls, sailing through a stormy sea; the blackness of darkness overhead; even the trusted captain of the craft, bewildered by the false signal lights of the wreckers of Wall street, has given orders for steering the craft upon a false course, and gone below. The underofficers of the ship, knowing the perfidy of his advisers, knowing that death and ruin are not six cable lengths ahead, deem it no disrespect to the honest commander in his absence to thwart the designs of the wreckers, assist in putting the helm hard over, and guiding the ship into a smooth and open sea. The members of this House are the second officers in command of the great Ship of State, and charged with equal responsibility for her safety.

The President knows, and every intelligent man must know, that the unconditional repeal of the Sherman act means a further fall in the price of silver bullion, and its utter destruction as a legal-tender metal in this country and all over the world. What, then, must be the opinion of the President touching the honesty and intelligence of those gentlemen on the floor of the House who, to justify themselves to an outraged constituency, state that they are in favor of free-silver coinage, but shall vote against any substitute to accompany the bill for repeal? You are in the attitude of old Pete Jones, who said, concerning a stringent liquor law, "I am in favor of yer law, but agin its enforcement." You are in favor of bimetallism; nevertheless, "tu Brute" art willing to give it the death-stab in the back. All humanity admire positive men and, even though they deem them wrong, honor those who have at all times and under all circumstances the courage of their conscientious convictions. But for the trimmer, the time server: Thus saith the Lord:

14 And unto the angel of the church of the Laodiceans write:

* * * * * * *

I know thy works, that thou art neither cold nor hot; I would thou wert cold or hot.

16 So then because thou art lukewarm, and neither cold nor hot, I will spew thee out of my mouth.

Mr. Speaker, that is our idea of about what the President must fee like telling some who hold their convictions as a stock of trading capital, and, whatever the opinion of the Executive, I am prone to the belief that, throughout the wheat and cotton belts a year hence, there will be a tremendous spewing of loads which rest heavily upon the stomachs of the producers.

I was in the country the other night, driving, and saw a sign stuck out on the side of the road, "Cash paid for hides." [Laughter and applause.] And along on the fence was a string of them, the tails hung over to the road; and I said to myself: "Are men going to sell not only their hides, but bodies, souls, conscience, moral obligations, and sense of duty, to steal from their families and throw them into despair and ruin, and not even get the cash price for it?" [Laughter and applause.] And I imagined, sir, that there would be seen a year from next November, by those who would ride through the rural highways, on the fences of the different sections of the agricultural communities, the hides of many so-called statesmen who think they can curry favor by fulsome fawning. [Laughter and applause.] I will take my chances of loss along those lines if you are willing to take yours. [Renewed laughter and applause.]

Mr. Speaker, the proposition is to repeal the Sherman act, without any attempt to carry out the other pledges of the platform, which demands the free and equal coinage of both gold and silver. Well, we want the Sherman law repealed. It is acknowledged by its author as a mere subterfuge adopted by the enemies of silver to prevent free coinage, which was demanded for the undoing of the villainy of 1873. Every man has joined in execrating that villainy and the villains, and they believe that along with the names of Judas Iscariot and Benedict Arnold will be placed those who were guilty of that crime; that in a blacker page of American history than that in which any American name has been written will be inscribed the authors of that monstrous crime.

We have denounced it, and yet to-day what are we asked to do? We are asked to say that all the Democrats of the past who drew up such platforms were unwise and unpatriotic; that they were mistaken. We have been told by members of this House, who profess to be Democrats, that this plank was made up of pure catchwords, and we are asked to say that there was one man of transcendent genius, who was twenty years ahead of his fellows, and we are asked here at this time and at this hour to come together and bend our knees and offer an apotheosis to that Senator, who sits enshrined at the other end of this Capitol Building. For one, I never will. [Applause.]

Mr. Speaker, when the Lord led the children of Israel out of captivity and the prophet, the leader, and the lawgiver had gone up into the mountain to meet the living God, these same people who to-day demand the unconditional repeal of the Sherman bill, these same people whose chief interests lie along in that direction, erected a golden calf and fell down and worshiped it; but the prophet of the Lord ground that calf into powder and spread it out upon the waters; and the Lord was sorely vexed with Israel because thereof. My friends, you can let them fall down and worship at this shrine. There may be many who still will worship at the shrine of Baal and Moloch, but there are still a majority of the citizens who know not these false gods.

I ask you, my friend, if you are a banker, if you are a manufacturer, an agriculturist, if you are a laboring man, if you own interests in railroads and draw dividends, or if you manage and conduct these affairs, when was your greatest era of prosperity? It was from 1866, or after the close of the war, down to 1873, was it not? Your railroad stocks were dividend payers at that time. You had no strikes, you had no boycotts, and no granger legislation. All classes of the people were at peace with each other. Your factories were not closed, and you did not have to call out armed forces to keep the employé from the throat of the employer.

Since 1873 what has been the history? Disaster has followed disaster as upon the speed of the whirlwind. The conditions have grown more strained every moment, and are growing more and more so with each recurring year. Statesmen and patriots may well ponder this condition. You have had warnings all along the past which show you the natural trend of such conditions. And now the people, the great producers of the world, come to you and ask for justice.

My farmer friend, when was it that you got $1.50 for your wheat, and when did you get 60 or 70 cents for your corn? In 1873 you received 118 cents per bushel, on an average, for wheat, and in 1873 your silver was demonetized. You planters and growers of cotton, tell me in what year was it that you received 23 cents a pound for your product? It was in 1873; but in that year we demonetized silver, and what happened? Why, we turned over the interests of the producers of this nation into the hands of British financiers. Let us look at it. Silver at that time was worth 129.29 cents per ounce; that was its coinage value. And at that time we had the grain markets and the cotton markets of the world; and in 1873 India exported only 735,000 bushels of wheat.

Now, there has never been a time in the history of India when silver has not been its money, and there has never been a time from the day when they commenced raising wheat down to the present hour that one ounce of silver did not measure the value of one bushel of wheat. It makes no difference what the value of the rupee is. The same number of rupees buy the same number of bushels of wheat all the time. But England could not afford to buy an ounce of silver at 129.29 and take it to India to measure the value of her wheat, so she took our wheat from us and paid us a little less, from 120 to 123 cents, in 1873.

Mr. BRYAN. Mr. Speaker, as the time of the gentleman from Pennsylvania [Mr. SIBLEY] has almost expired, I ask unanimous consent that he be permitted to conclude his remarks without limit.

There was no objection, and it was so ordered.

Mr. SIBLEY. Mr. Speaker, I thank the members of the House for their courtesy.

In 1874 the shipments of wheat from India commenced. England bought her ounce of silver here at 110 cents, and she could take that to India and exchange it for a bushel of Indian wheat; and in five years after the demonetization of silver, England had increased her shipments from 735,000 bushels to 11,900,000 bushels.

In ten years, with the continuous depreciation in the value of silver, the shipments of Indian wheat had increased from 11,000,000 to 26,000,000 bushels. In fifteen years the shipments of Indian wheat to Europe had increased from 735,000 bushels in 1873 to 41,000,000 bushels, and last year she exported 59,000,000 bushels. The same ounce of silver England could not buy, to develop the grain markets of India, at less than 129 cents, before this demonetization and hostile legislation, she now buys at 70 cents, and takes it to India and still gets the same bushel of wheat for it, as when silver was worth $1.10. We have played all these years into the hands of England against the prosperity of our own American wheat producers. And yet some gentlemen from the Mississippi Valley and from the great wheat-growing States come here and say that this metal must go lower still in order that their constituents may continue to feed the European nations at even a less price than they are able to command to-day.

Mr. Speaker, let us look at cotton, and see if the analogy does not hold true there also. They established cotton mills in India in 1863, and from that year down to 1874 they were never able to export one pound of cotton yarn; eleven years of attempts to introduce cotton-spinning in India, with abject failure as the result. But in 1874, one year after the demonetization of silver, they shipped 1,000,000 pounds of cotton yarn. The next year they shipped 5,000,000 pounds. With each decreasing quotation in the value of the ounce of silver bullion there was an increase in the export of cotton yarn from India. In 1889 it had gone up to 65,000,000 pounds.

In 1891, the last year for which I have been able to secure figures, the exports of cotton yarn from India amounted to 165,000,000 pounds; the same thing has been equally true of the exports of raw cotton. Mr. Speaker, I have observed that the prosperity of the farmers and the railroads went hand in hand, and are there no lessons that the managers and stockholders of railroads can learn from these conditions above described? Which is better for your corporations, to be able to earn money at the expense of Europe or to be able to borrow it from Europe at your own expense? Permit me to show the position of those in England who are so much opposed to bimetallism. At a meeting of the British and Colonial Chambers of Commerce, held in London in 1886, Sir Robert N. Fowler, a member of Parliament, a banker, and an ex-mayor of London, said—

that the effect of the depreciation of silver must finally be the ruin of the wheat and cotton industries of America, and be the development of India as the chief wheat and cotton exporter of the world.

Russia, another silver nation, and the great competitor of America in the production of wheat, has also furnished to European nations her quota of wheat, paid for in the depreciated ounce of silver that we by legislation have degraded and debased. Oh, I tell you, my friends, it is very fine to hear you talk here about a "degraded and debased dollar;" but I would rather have a degraded dollar than a degraded country—rather have a debased coin than a debased people. You have closed the market to American wheat and American cotton; and yet gentlemen from the cotton States stand here and say that the cotton-planter demands that the Sherman act shall be repealed.

The people of the cotton States, I believe, are equal in intelligence to the people of the wheat-producing States and the other great States of this Union where greed for gain and lust for riches are not the one dominating and controlling force. You have seen your cotton crop increase. I will not take time to go into statistics as to the acreage; but you have planted millions more of acres; you have raised hundreds of millions more pounds of cotton; and your net receipts to-day are not one-half what they were in 1873. Every year a little greater shrinkage in value because of the shrinkage of value of silver bullion.

Now, I want to make my friend from Ohio [Mr. HARTER] a proposition. I know he is out for converts. I know the corridors of this Capitol are thronged with a lobby that are trying to make converts; and the hotels are full of them. Now, I want to tell the gentleman how he can make one convert right here. I make this proposition: That silver has not declined in value one iota from 1873 down to this minute; if it has, I will vote on the other side of this proposition. It has maintained its parity and its ratio with every product of human industry, save one. This ounce of bullion silver which to-day you tell me is worth but 70 cents, measures as much wheat and more than it ever measured in the last fifty years; it measures more pounds of beef, more pounds of pork, more pounds of cotton, more pounds of iron, more barrels of oil, more of every product of human industry, save one, than it ever measured even when it sold at its legitimate value, 129 cents an ounce. If you will show me any other than one exception to this proposition, you have a convert right here. The one exception is gold. The 70 cent ounce of silver will not buy as much gold to-day, but it will buy more of every other product of human industry.

Now, then, inasmuch as silver has maintained its ratio—its parity with your wheat, and your corn, and your cotton, with every product of human labor, why do you say that silver has gone down and that this metal is debased? Why do you not say that gold has gone up and has been deified? You cry out in these Halls for an "honest dollar." You do not want an honest dollar—not one of you that makes this cry. [Applause.] You want a scarce dollar. You do not want an honest dollar; if you do, come over and vote with us, and we will give it to you. [Applause.] We will give you a dollar that is as honest to day as it was in 1873. But you are not going to force your 150-cent dishonest dollar upon the great producers of the necessities of human existence—not if we can prevent the consummation of that effort. [Applause.] Talk about a dishonest silver dollar, when within the last week they have been so scarce as to command a premium of 2 and 3 per cent to assist in moving the cotton and wheat crops.

I love to hear gentlemen talk about "intrinsic value." That word "intrinsic" has a golden sound. I do not know what it means, and I do not think anyone else does; but I will give you my idea of intrinsic value. The intrinsic value of anything is what it will do for you in your hour of direst need, of supremest peril. What is the intrinsic value of a piece of plank 24 feet long, a foot wide, and 2 inches thick? Gentlemen may take out their pencils and commence to figure out the intrinsic value of that piece of plank, and their results will vary according to their methods of computation; but, my friends, the intrinsic value of that plank is a million dollars to the man who is drowning.

Men talk about the intrinsic value of gold. A banker told me the other day that he could not assent to my propositions because he believed the time had come when we must join hands with the other great nations and come down to the use of a metal which had intrinsic value behind it. I said to this gentleman: "I do not know that I can raise the funds just at present; I have serious doubts if I can raise a percentage of the amount; but suppose I can get $20,000 worth of gold bullion. You pay 3 per cent on time deposits, do you not?" "Yes, sir." "Well, now I will get $20,000 worth of gold bullion and bring it to you as a deposit. You would rather have that than paper, because paper has no intrinsic value, while gold bullion has. I will deposit this bullion for six months and draw 3 per cent interest on this time deposit." What do you think he said? "Oh," said he, "I can not give you 3 per cent on that." "Why not," said I? "Well, I could not use it." "Well, then," said I, "I will take the bullion down to the mint at Philadelphia and I will get the people there to put upon it the stamp and superscription of the Government of the United States; will you take it then?" He said: "Oh, yes; I would be glad to." "Well, then," said I, "what has your intrinsic value got to do with the matter? What is it gives this metal its power as money so that you are willing to pay me 3 per cent interest upon it? Is it the intrinsic value of the metal? No; it is the image and superscription of Cæsar that makes it money?"

I have been amused to hear gentlemen talk about the impossibility and absurdity of having two yardsticks. Well, my friends, I believe we have two yardsticks. I believe that when you attempt to appreciate gold we will set silver against it at 129 cents an ounce, and we will hold it so that the gold dollar shall be worth just 100 cents; and the gold dollar shall sustain the silver dollar so that it shall stand at 100 cents; so that we can have two measures for the same thing. Why, sir, 32 quarts of oats make a bushel, do they not? And 32 pounds of oats make a bushel. There you have two yardsticks, have you not?

Now these measures are of the same ratio. But 32 quarts of corn make a bushel, and 56 pounds of corn make a bushel. There is the varying ratio. There are 60 pounds of wheat in a bushel, but only 32 quarts. Is there any great discrepancy in using the two measures? Why, one says the seller shall not take a hoop and scoop out down below the level of the rim, and the other says the man who buys it shall not heap up the measure to running over. That is what it is. That is why we place one coin against the other.

Now, my friends say that silver has gone down all over the nations of the world, and that it can not be maintained at a parity or fixed ratio. No wonder it has gone down. What criminal has ever been pursued with such zealous and malignant fury, such thorough and complete conspiracy? What criminal has ever been followed with such relentless hatred? The energies of the entire money power of the whole world have been concentrated against the white metal. Why has this been done? Because they were afraid it was going to be too abundant. The Creator in his loving kindness to this nation, when the foundations of the world were laid, stored our mountains and our hills with great veins of silver and gold, that ought to make us the greatest, the grandest, the noblest, the richest nation on earth, in order that we might enlighten, civilize, and carry glad tidings of great joy to all the dwellers of the earth. They became afraid of the quantity of silver in this country, just as they were frightened about gold in 1857; the only difference was that they got afraid of a different thing.

The discovery of the gold mines of Australia in 1853, following the discovery of those in California in 1849, made these same gold bugs fear that there was going to be too much gold, and they called their monetary conferences together to conspire against gold. They used then precisely the same arguments against gold that they have directed against silver at the present time, and they had a better argument. They said silver was the money of the common people, adapted to the transaction of small business as well as great; that the people could use it freely and safely; that its size was such as to make it a safer metal for many purposes, and that the loss by abrasion in silver coin was so little and in gold so much that gold ought never to have been made a money metal at all; and that the gold should be used only as bullion and have a basic value.

Listening to this series of arguments which have been put forth by those men who desire to control all human industries and values, several nations in Europe did demonetize gold and take away its legal-tender value no longer ago than 1857. Austria demonetized it, and every state of Germany demonetized it; and now we are told this debased metal, silver, ought to be demonetized merely because they are afraid of such an abundance of it!

What wonder that it is disgraced when every factor, every power not only of the whole American continent but all the world, has been used against it? Your banks have denounced it. Your metropolitan press, under the control of the gold power, have issued column after column attacking it. Your very Director of the Mint, or Acting Director, has discredited it within the last four weeks. He has wiggled and haggled over the price and value of it, and if the holders offered it at 70.71 cents an ounce he would offer them 70.31 cents an ounce. When still lacking 2,000,000 of ounces to comply with the plain terms of the law he would, when his offer was accepted, take 30,000 ounces instead of half a million. Instead of, as an American, being animated by an impulse to maintain its value at parity if possible, he pursued methods which in this nation seldom obtain outside the second-hand clothing shops of Baxter street. That certain elements have conspired against it to degrade it and take away its value in this country, who can longer doubt?

Mr. Speaker, let us place the responsibility for this panic where it belongs. India closed her mints to the free coinage of silver a few weeks ago; and I want to call your attention in this connection to a reputed interview which had a dominating and controlling force in that direction. A member of the Administration, the Secretary of Agriculture of this Union, ostensibly at the head of the agriculturists of the nation and who is said at times to imagine he hears the Presidential bee buzzing in his bonnet, was interviewed a few weeks ago, and in that interview he is reported to have said: "I have recommended to the Secretary of the Treasury that he condemn all the silver in the vaults of the Government and sell it as old junk, for whatever it will bring." He said, "We have a law which allows the appointment of committees to condemn worthless material lying around the Departments." And three days after that interview silver was demonetized in India.

Whether the Secretary of Agriculture spoke seriously or in jest, we know not. If this was a jest it was one that has cost more closing of banks, more foreclosures upon farms and houses, closed more workshops, put out more fires in happy homes, caused more loss, more hunger, more tears, more misery, more woe, than any jest ever recorded on the pages of the past. The utterances of cabinet ministers are supposed to be those of deliberation, and the result of fullest consideration, and presumptively reflecting and outlining governmental policy.

What wonder in the face of such declarations, made upon the authority of one holding so exalted and dignified a position, that the British ministry was suddenly convened to protect the Indian mints from such an avalanche; and from that moment to this, disaster has trod upon the heels of disaster, ever thicker, ever faster. Such sorry jests should entitle the discoverer of Arbor Day to an indefinite leave of absence, where, beneath the umbrageous foliage of his planting, he may repent his costly folly. Silver fell from 83½ cents per ounce to 70 cents as the result of this man's utterance; and wheat, always following the price of silver, declined from 74 cents per bushel to 54 cents per bushel.

A few days since our worthy Secretary was interviewed again, and this is his latest reported utterance of financial wisdom:

> Agricultural products are lower, but this is rather a blessing than otherwise, for if our products are not taken gold will be exported.

This utterance, if correct, ought to make it all right with the farmers, who care nothing whatsoever about the price of the products of their toil, so that the yellow god may not flee from the presence of his devout worshipers.

Mr. Speaker, the farmers have for years been great sufferers from the ravages of bugs. You of the South have had the cotton bug. You of the West have had the chinch bug. We of the North have had the potato bug, and scattered around promiscuously has been the bedbug; but indigenous to Lombard and Wall streets, thrives and fattens another bug. They even break their way into this Capitol at times, and these bugs—gold bugs—have bitten and annoyed more people than all the bedbug tribe, and their ravages in your fertile fields exceed in damage in a single year the damage wrought by the combined efforts of all other bugs for a century.

Mr. Speaker, I like the gentleman from Ohio [Mr. HARTER]. He has got such a frank, manly way of stating things. He states a proposition squarely and fairly, while many others are apt to hedge. He admits the question to-day to be this: Silver is going to be money equal in value to gold in this country, and that issue is to be determined now; or silver, its money value, is to be absolutely lost forever. I like the way he states his propositions. He says squarely that to-day we have too much money, and therefore he proposes to take away one-half of it.

Why do not some others stand up on this floor, and say publicly what they say in private conversation? Why do you not announce your intention manfully and boldly from your places here? You have announced privately that your intention is to offer resolutions, after the repeal of the Sherman law, to take away the legal-tender power of silver in all sums in excess of five dollars. Why do you not tell what justification you are going to offer for that? Privately, you say you are going to justify it by the fact that when you have unconditionally repealed this bill, silver will fall to forty cents an ounce or even less, and then you can urge the folly of putting out a twenty-five cent silver dollar and making it a full legal tender.

Why, my friends, the great temple of industry and commerce rests upon two pillars, one of silver and the other of gold. This one of silver has but 6 per cent more strength than the other, and with both these pillars under this temple it is all it can do to maintain its place. Why, every passing financial wind rocks it upon its foundations; and yet you propose to absolutely destroy one of these pillars. There is only 6 per cent more silver on the whole globe than of gold; only $2.58 per capita of silver in the world. Yet you propose to take it away. Over three-fifths of the nations of the world to-day are either upon a silver or a bimetallic basis. Your $3,600,000,000 of gold is inadequate for the use of the nations that are already upon a gold standard, and how are you going to move the wheels of industry when you have destroyed one-half the metallic base of all commercial credits and transactions, the globe around?

But they cite England, old England, and Spain and Germany. Yet they dodge the issue. There is just one country on the face of the globe where they do not have panics, and she has got more money than any other civilized nation on the face of the globe, and that country is France. No financial revolutions or panics or disasters there. The Panama Canal scheme may fail, and it does not make a ripple on the financial surface. It causes great waves to heave and swell upon the political tide, but it never touches the financial situation or affects its stability. They have $54 of money to every man, woman, and child in France. They have an abundance to meet the needs of business in that little nation, smaller than some of our States; and yet in this great nation, whose territory stretches 3,000 miles from ocean to ocean, we are asked to do business with less than half as much per capita. If silver makes panics, why was it that Australia, which is on a gold basis, has a panic worse than ours; a panic in which the bank failures in six weeks amount to over nine hundred millions of dollars? Their panic was only caused, like ours, by Rothschild shearing his sheep.

My friend, let us deal fairly with silver. Supposing that by your legislation here to-morrow you enact a law that no man in this country who possesses wheat shall be permitted to take it to the mill and have it ground. Shut every mill in the land to the grinding of wheat, and what do you think wheat would be worth six months from to-day? Do you think wheat would maintain its value as silver has done? Corn would go up, corn would be king, and wheat would be worth its fodder value for dumb brutes. That is precisely what you have done against silver. You have shut down the mills against it. You have denied it to the public for its use, and yet you cry against it that there are only 53 or 56 cents in the silver dollar.

Now, my friends, I want to make you a little prediction right here, and let us see who tells you the truth, whether it is these people from New York or the friends of free coinage. Oh, I love the New York people! I know them well. It is the State of my nativity. There are grand men and noble women in New York. But I know New York City well, and I know, lying right alongside of New York City, is a place they call Hell Gate, and I think most of you, coming from there, have been through it. [Laughter.] I know our friends from New England, who speak so boldly for the honest dollar, in coming through the Sound, have come through Hell Gate. [Laughter.]

But I want to tell you, my friends, that we have been getting the financial policy of this nation for twenty years from the gates of hell, but we are not going to accept such dictum any longer. [Applause.] Why, did you ever stop to think that when the wise men started out to seek the Saviour of mankind, the Light of the World, in what direction they traveled? Did they go to the East to look for the light? No; they left the East and came to the West for the source and fountain of all light and truth. [Laughter and applause.]

When Columbus embarked, in which direction did he steer to find a nobler, better, and happier land? Did he turn to the East? No! Misery, woe, monarchs, oppression, crime, and crowns were in the East. He headed his course westward; and so, my friends, to-day you will never find a financial savior who comes up through Hell Gate. [Laughter.] On this rock of justice we have founded our faith, and the gates of hell shall not prevail against us. [Laughter.] They have told us about the great loss that the country submitted to in the purchase of silver, and I want to say right here, my friends, first, that I used to be a monometallist of the monometallists; could not be anything else. All my friends were monometallists. I was a director in a national bank, and they were all monometallists.

Everybody I met in the East was a monometallist. But I one day heard a man talk who astonished me. He read from official documents, and I doubted their accuracy. I said, "That man has the appearance of honesty; he has the courage of truth shining from his soul through his eyes, but he must be mistaken." So I said, "For my part I am going to make a study of this question." And never thinking to be here in political debate and discussion within these Halls, or any other public place, I devoted my time to studying these questions. I sent here to Washington for the reports of your Director of the Mint, Comptroller of the Currency, and Treasurer, and tried to apply business rules and methods to them, and I am no longer a monometallist, because I would rather be honest than be a monometallist. [Laughter and applause.]

My friends, we are told that the Treasury, and the country through the Treasury, has lost vast sums of money in buying 70-cent silver and storing it in our vaults. Now, let us see the facts about that. Maybe we have been driving a better trade than we thought. If that bullion has gone into dollars it will pay the Government's debts. It has done so up to this time, at least, but I do not know what it will do if you succeed in your schemes, but up to this time it will pay a dollar's worth of debt, public or private, anywhere in the nation when it is coined into standard silver dollars.

How much have we lost? Have we lost anything? Every ounce in the Treasury bought below $1.29 an ounce, its coinage value, is so much gain. Instead of issuing bulletins to the people showing the great loss in the purchase of silver, why do not they say that the Government is 50 cents ahead on every ounce of silver that it has purchased, and that the Government is $100,000,00 ahead by the purchase of silver, instead of sending out reports that the Government has been a loser by the transaction?

But supposing we had been loser. Supposing, Mr. Speaker, that we had as a Government chartered one of the ocean greyhounds sailing from New York and had loaded every ounce of silver in the country that has been produced since 1873 to the present time, had bought that silver for $1.29 an ounce, and had that ship to sail just off beyond the banks of Newfoundland, and gone into sufficiently deep water where you could not reach soundings, and sunk it to the depths of the ocean, where it would have remained forever beyond the reach of man, what would have been the effect on the producers of the United States?

The highest production of silver in any year has been $73,000,000. We will say it is $75,000,000. But we produce 450,000,000 bushels of wheat a year, which, since the demonetization of silver, has fallen from $1.20 to 54 cents per bushel. The American farmers have lost from 60 to 70 cents a bushel on wheat. The price has gone down because England can come here and take 70 cents' worth of silver and measure it against a bushel of wheat in India, just as well as she could do when it was worth $1.29 before we demonetized it by legislation, and degraded and disgraced it by our silly and wicked follies. Now, then, Mr. Speaker, we have a loss of 50 cents a bushel on wheat—I want to make my statement modest. We have a loss of 50 cents a bushel on 450,000,000 bushels of wheat a year, which makes a loss to the American farmer of $225,000,000.

I am not here talking for the silver mine owners of Idaho, Colorado, Nevada, Montana, and Utah. I do not know them. They are only a small factor in this question. I am looking to the producers of wheat and corn, cotton and tobacco, and all the wealth of the nation. We have lost $225,000,000 each year in the value of wheat. Why, if we had bought that 75,000,000 ounces of silver and sunk it in the depths of the sea, so that England could not have got it at 70 cents an ounce, the American wheat-grower would have been a gainer of $225,000,000 annually. We produce 2,000,000 000 bushels of corn, and corn has fallen 26 cents a bushel. Wheat is the great staple, the great leader, and corn is but a follower of wheat among the cereals. Now, then, I will say that we lost 20 cents a bushel on corn; and so our American growers of corn have lost $400,000,000 annually upon their crop of corn, so that if they had bought all this silver and sunk it the corn-growers would have been $325,000,000 to the good.

We produce 3,212,000,000 pounds of cotton annually, and in 1873 your cotton sold at 22 cents a pound. To-day it is bringing 7 and 8 cents. You have lost 12 cents a pound on every pound of cotton; and if the cotton-producers had bought all the silver and sunk it in the depths of the ocean they would have been each year $210,000,000 ahead on the transaction. In these three leading articles of production in the Union (I will not go through more of them) the loss to the producer each year has been $910,000,000 more than the value of the silver that it would have been necessary to have purchased.

Oh, my friends, they argue against silver. They say that our legislation is for the benefit of a few mine owners. Why, they are the most insignificant factor in the whole problem, although by their industry they have added to our wealth $75,000,000 annually. But this is a drop in the bucket, and yet we can afford to be just, even though they are not a great factor. I sat in Chicago at the Auditorium Hotel a few days ago conversing with a gentleman. I noticed that he was looking rather blue. He finally reached me a copy of the Chicago Tribune, and said: "Mr. Sibley, I want to call your attention to one fact. Here is a statement made, as by authority, showing the cost of production of silver. They have taken the leading mines, and have figured it out here that it only costs 40 cents an ounce to produce it. Now," he says, "I want you to look at that mine, where they say the cost is only 40 cents an ounce. Four weeks ago we took our pumps out of that mine, and the water covers our levels to-day, and there never will be an ounce of silver produced from that mine again. The average cost of mining of silver in that mine is much more than $1 an ounce; and we have been running it for the last few years, hoping and praying for better times, until we could get our money out of the production." It is unfair to take four or five of the leading mines in silver producing and, taking the cost of production in those mines, say that that is the cost of the production of silver. It is just as unfair as it would be to come to us in our Commonwealth and take four or five producers of petroleum whose wells yield 300, 500, and even 10,000 barrels a day, and assume that petroleum only costs 10 cents a barrel to produce, because these men who are producing thousands of barrels a day may be making a profit.

To-day the market for petroleum in Pennsylvania is 58 cents, and for two years it has been produced at a loss of not less than 10 cents a barrel. You say, "Then, why don't they shut down?" Why, their case is like that of the fellow who had hold of the bear's tail and wanted some one to help him let go. [Laughter.] If they close down those wells the salt water will flood them, and the oil will never come again; so, in desperation, they have held on to their little wells and pumped them at a loss, waiting and praying for the better times which the Democratic platform promised to give the country. [Applause.]

Now, let us deal fairly with silver. Statistics that are in the hands of gentlemen upon this floor—as authoritative statistics, I presume, as those of the Treasury Department—show that the average cost of production of an ounce of silver has been nearer to $2 than to $1.

Mr. PENCE. If the gentleman will pardon the interruption, I will state to the House, by way of illustrating the point he is making, that the report of the Senate Committee on Mining, which was made to the Senate last March, but is not yet, I believe, generally in the hands of members here, shows that the cost of production of gold and silver is more than its coinage value. Let me say, further, that the verified records show that in the most important silver mining camp in the world, Leadville, Lake County, Colo., where the silver mining industry began in 1879, there were located, recorded, and worked, from 1879 to June 1 of this year, 19,300 mining locations. Upon each of them an average of ten acres, $100 worth of work has been done, at an average cost of $10 per acre. The result has been that but 3,800 of them have been considered of sufficient value to be patented, and for the last twelve months but eighteen of those mines have been worked at a profit. I present these figures as illustrating the gentleman's point.

Mr. SIBLEY. I am much obliged to the gentleman.

Mr. PICKLER [to Mr. SIBLEY]. Will you discuss the ratio before you close?

Mr. SIBLEY. Mr. Speaker, a gentleman near me asks me to discuss the question of the ratio before I sit down. I am not particular about the ratio, but I would rather see it 15½ to 1 than 16 to 1, because I would rather see the people get 11 or 12 cents a pound for their cotton, and $1.10 a bushel for their wheat. I would rather see the ratio 16 to 1 than 17 to 1, because if the people are to be robbed at all I would rather they were robbed of ten cents than of twenty.

I will agree to a ratio of 18 to 1 upon the same principle. I will agree to a ratio of 20 to 1, because I would rather see the farmers get 65 or 70 cents a bushel for their wheat than that they should be compelled to take the price they will get the day you pass this measure of repeal without providing a substitute for the existing law. I will make this prophecy, and we shall see who prophesies correctly: The day you repeal the Sherman act, or within four weeks from that time, if you repeal it without a substitute, silver will strike 45 or 50 cents an ounce and wheat will sell below 45 cents a bushel. When silver strikes 40 cents an ounce your cotton will strike 4 cents a pound.

What had England to gain by stopping the mintage of silver in India? The two great English political parties, the Conservatives and the Liberals, are very evenly divided, and although the gentleman from Ohio [Mr. HARTER] has talked so eloquently about the happiness and prosperity of England, yet we know that for three years past ruin, distress, and starvation have prevailed there. The Liberal party, in order that it might maintain itself in power, jumped at the occasion to stop the silver mintage in India, depressing the price from 82½ to 70 cents an ounce, and you saw how the wheat market followed it from 75 cents to 53 cents per bushel.

You never saw the day when silver went up that wheat did not go up, and cotton also. We know that after the passage of the Sherman law, which men said was going to remedy the then existing evils, silver bounded to 120 cents an ounce, and wheat bounded up with it. If you give us free-silver coinage at a ratio of 16 to 1 we, as the friends of silver, are ready to-day to pledge our faith to the farmers of the West and the cotton-growers of the South that they will get 11 cents a pound for their cotton and $1.10 for their wheat.

Mr. HICKS. May I ask the gentleman a question?

Mr. SIBLEY. Yes, sir.

Mr. HICKS. If limited coinage has reduced the price of wheat in Pennsylvania to 60 cents a bushel, how does the gentleman make out that free and unlimited coinage will raise it to a dollar?

Mr. SIBLEY. Because of the ability of England to take the ounce of silver which she buys here at 70 cents, and go to India and buy as much wheat with it as she ever could buy at any time with an ounce of silver. As I have said, the ounce of silver still measures the value of the bushel of wheat in India. If she has to pay us, as she will under a free-coinage act with a ratio of 16 to 1, $1.29 an ounce for silver, she can not take it to India to exchange for wheat, but must come to us and pay a dollar or more for wheat.

A MEMBER. Laid down in Liverpool?

Mr. SIBLEY. Yes.

Mr. HICKS. One more question. What was the price of wheat when the Sherman law was enacted?

Mr. SIBLEY. Do you mean the law of 1890?

Mr. HICKS. Yes.

Mr. SIBLEY. Eighty-three cents.

Mr. HICKS. What is it worth to-day?

Mr. SIBLEY. It sold last week at 53 cents in Chicago.

Mr. COX It has sold in South Tennessee for 38 cents.

Mr. HICKS. Now, will the gentleman please answer this question: If limited coinage has reduced the price of wheat from 83 to 53 cents, how can free and unlimited coinage raise the price?

Mr. SIBLEY. Mr. Speaker, I think that is a fair question. We have not had any coinage in the proper sense; we have not coined our silver; we have denied its money value; we have debased it and degraded it and have made it a tool for England to use to destroy the wheat-growers and cotton-growers of this nation. We have coined only a part. Free coinage will do this: You coin fifty-four millions out of a production of seventy-five millions, and the twenty-one millions of surplus determines the value of the balance.

We have said that $54,000,000 of this is money and the balance pig metal; and it has been the pig metal that has fixed the prices all the time, and not the money. I invite the lawyers of this body to jump on that proposition, if they can. The lawyers and the bankers are standing together here pretty solid. [Laughter.] The lawyers came on one occasion to the incarnate God, and thought to confuse him by asking some questions; and I remember he turned to them and said:

Woe unto you also, ye lawyers! for ye lade men with burdens grievous to be borne, and ye yourselves touch not the burdens with one of your fingers.

Woe unto you, lawyers! for ye have taken away the key of knowledge: ye entered not in yourselves, and them that were entering in ye hindered.

[Applause.]

Mr. HICKS. I would like to ask the gentleman another question. He has said, as I understand, that it is the pig-metal silver that has regulated the price of wheat. Am I correct in understanding him that way?

Mr. SIBLEY. I did not catch the gentleman's remark.

Mr. HICKS. Do you say that the price of the pig metal regulates the price of wheat?

Mr. SIBLEY. I say that the price of this disgraced, debased, decried surplus has regulated the value of wheat at all times since 1873. I will maintain that proposition at any and all hazards.

Mr. HICKS. For every bar of silver that has been placed in the Treasury silver notes have been issued, have they not?

Mr. SIBLEY. I do not know that there has been a silver note issued for every bar. I can tell the gentleman the exact amount in a moment if he desires.

Mr. HICKS. I understood the gentleman to say that the silver is lying idle in the Treasury; but I also understand that a note has been issued representing every dollar's worth of silver that is in the Treasury.

Mr. SIBLEY. It is the amount that has not come into the Treasury that has caused the distress to the farmers and producers of this nation.

Mr. HICKS. I am a farmer like yourself, and I am also a lawyer. I farm at long range, just as you do. I am very anxious, however, to know how the repeal of the Sherman law can in any way affect the price of wheat or raise the value of farm lands. If you can convince me that free and unlimited coinage will have the effect that you state, I am ready to vote for it.

Mr. SIBLEY. Well, I am going to convert you right now, if you will stand by your proposition. [Laughter.]

Mr. HICKS. All right.

Mr. SIBLEY. We can only judge of the future by the past and the present. Everything has declined since you demonetized silver, since you commenced hostile legislation against it. Pennsylvania farm lands to-day are not worth 40 cents upon the dollar of what they were in 1873. Is not that correct?

Mr. HICKS. I am sorry to say it is the fact.

Mr. SIBLEY. And none of the products of the Pennsylvania farm—your wheat and corn and beef—bear a higher ratio than that, compared with the price in 1873; is not that the fact? Now, then, we know that something happened in 1873, that permitted England to come here and buy an ounce of silver at 70 or 80 or 90 cents and take it to India and exchange it for a bushel of wheat. And that very fact—that we have not given silver the place that rightfully belongs to it as one of the precious metals of the earth, as one of the foundations of credit, has enabled her to use that depreciated metal—which if we had free silver coinage would at all times be worth 129 cents an ounce—has enabled England to come here and get this metal at 90 cents an ounce, and with it purchase wheat and cotton to come into competition with our products. For the information of the gentleman let me send to the desk to be read an extract from the language of Archbishop Walsh of Dublin.

The Clerk read as follows:

The classic prediction in this matter is that of the French economist, M. Ernest Seyd. So far back as 1871, two years before the calamitous success of the doctrinaire crusade against the maintenance of the bimetallist system as it was then in operation in France, M. Seyd used the following remarkable words:

"It is a great mistake to suppose that the adoption of the gold (standard of value) by other States besides England will be beneficial. It will only lead to the destruction of the monetary equilibrium hitherto existing, and cause a fall in the value of silver from which England's trade and the Indian silver valuations will suffer more than all other interests, grievous as the general decline of prosperity all over the world will be."

Then comes a singularly noteworthy passage:

The strong doctrinairism existing in England as regards the gold valuation is so blind that, when the time of depression sets in, there will be this special feature:
The economical authorities of the country will refuse to listen to the cause here foreshadowed; every possible attempt will be made to prove that the decline of commerce is due to all sorts of causes and irreconcilable matters; the workman and his strikes will be the first convenient target; then "speculating" and "overtrading" will have their turn; many other allegations will be made, totally irrelevant to the real issue, but satisfactory to the moralizing tendency of financial writers.

Mr. BRYAN. May I interrupt the gentleman from Pennsylvania [Mr. SIBLEY] a moment?

Mr. SIBLEY. Certainly.

Mr. BRYAN. I would like to read in support of the gentleman's position an extract from the agricultural report of 1890, page 8—a report issued by Mr. Harrison's administration:

The recent legislation looking to the restoration of the bimetallic standard of our currency, and the consequent enhancement of the value of silver, has unquestionably had much to do with the recent advance in the price of cereals. The same cause has advanced the price of wheat in Russia and India, and in the same degree reduced their power of competition. English gold was formerly exchanged for cheap silver, and wheat purchased with the cheaper metal was sold in Great Britain for gold. Much of this advantage is lost by the appreciation of silver in those countries. It is reasonable, therefore, to expect much higher prices for wheat than have been received in recent years.

Mr. OUTHWAITE. Will the gentleman from Nebraska answer a question?

Mr. BRYAN. Yes, sir.

Mr. OUTHWAITE. Where was this cheap wheat, to which you refer, bought?

Mr. BRYAN. What cheap wheat?

Mr. OUTHWAITE. The cheap wheat that is alluded to in that article.

Mr. BRYAN. In Russia and India.

Mr. OUTHWAITE. What was the currency used in payment at that time?

Mr. BRYAN. Silver. But, let me say to the gentleman, the silver price was as high in India then as it is now—that is to say, it was as high in 1873—while the gold price has gone down in this country just as silver has gone down.

Mr. OUTHWAITE. In other words, they got a silver price for silver wheat.

Mr. BRYAN. I was only giving the article as it appears in this report; gentlemen can draw their own conclusions.

Mr. SIBLEY. Mr. Speaker, when I was interrupted first I was about to state the reasons that England desired, especially at that time, to depreciate further the value of silver. Parties were very evenly divided in Great Britain, and in order to maintain a majority Mr. Gladstone found it necessary to feed their people with cheaper food, to be able to put on the markets of England wheat at a lower price, and they accomplished their purpose by shutting up the coinage of silver in the India mint, and made the difference in price between 75 cents and 53 cents per bushel in the cost of wheat.

But you fear that she will not restore the coinage of silver to India. Not the slightest trouble about that. Why did she not put India on a gold basis? She did not allow the gold dollar or an ounce of gold to become a legal tender in India. Let her throw India open to gold coinage, and the whole problem will be solved, and we will not care what disposition we make of this question. Why it will solve the whole thing in a moment. It will solve itself. There would be no longer a problem as to where India would be.

Mr. Speaker, I have been amused at the attitude of Eastern Democrats on this question. I had to smile the day before yesterday when the gentleman from Ohio [Mr. GROSVENOR] spoke. If I ever heard the old Democratic party ripped up the back, jumped on, trampled on, shaken up, rolled all over the floor, he did it. [Laughter.] But when he wound up his speech with a declaration that as things were he thought he would vote for the unconditional repeal of the Sherman act, I saw one of my Democratic friends on this floor from New York clap his hands long and loud after everybody else had got through; and I could not tell whether he was applauding the first part of the gentleman's speech or the second part. [Laughter and applause.]

Mr. BRYAN. May I interrupt the gentleman from Pennsylvania long enough to insert in the RECORD in this connection what that gentleman from Ohio said in regard to the Sherman bill three years ago?

Mr. SIBLEY. Yes, sir.

Mr. BRYAN. On the 12th day of June, 1890, the gentleman from Ohio just referred to said on this floor:

The Republican party, true to its faithful guardianship of the people's interests, has determined to give to the people of the country a great increase in the circulation, and you resist, you refuse to have it.

Mr. SIBLEY. They tell us, Mr. Speaker, that if we adopt free-silver coinage at any ratio, or re-enact the Bland bill, gold will go out of the country. Well, now, we are not to be forever frightened by the bugaboo of gold. Suppose it does go out of the country. Nations are merely aggregations of individuals, and are governed by much the same laws, the same ideas, and rules that control individuals. No man gets a dollar of gold out of my pocket that I do not think I get an equivalent for in some way, shape, or form. Other countries will not get the gold from us unless they have something to give us that we would rather have than the gold. They must have something to exchange for our gold. And supposing that it does go out and they take it all. What then? They do not want to do it. They hold too many of our bonds, that under the present law are payable in coin of standard value, which means either silver or gold, to run any risks. They want gold in payment of these bonds, and they do not want all the gold to go from our country. But supposing again, I say, they take it all.

Why, what will happen then? They say gold will go to a premium. Well, it has been to a premium for twenty years, and you did not know it. Let it go to a premium, and when the Ward McAllisters and the other Four Hundred want to go to Europe for their summer outings, it will cost them a little more to make their exchanges, and if they bring home fine clothes, the products of European countries, it will cost them a good deal more money; and we will build a better tariff wall round our industries than that builded by the gentleman from Ohio. Why, if they will not take our money, we will not take their goods.

What trade will we lose? What nations do we wish to trade with? England, Germany, and France will not buy a dollar's worth of products of American labor. They take only the necessities of life, our wheat, our pork, our corn, and our cotton and beef; those they have got to have anyway, and they must pay us in the money we specify. Now, suppose they will not take our money. We will just stop buying of them, and that will start our own factories running, start our own spindles to humming and our own wheels to revolving.

Why, Mr. Speaker, as a man who is somewhat interested in a bank, and wishing to protect it, I say that for the safety of the small banker there is but one course, and that is bimetallism in this country. And whenever you make the foundation too narrow, whenever you set up the great pyramid upon its apex, and build up thereon, the higher you build the greater will be the ruin when some adverse circumstance runs up against your pyramid. You build it on a single standard, and your foundation is too narrow for safety, and whenever a wave of distrust runs over the country your little savings of a lifetime will be swept away.

The census showed that in 1890 twenty-four thousand people owned one-half of the total wealth of the nation; and since the shaking up you have given us over in New York the probabilities are that about fourteen thousand have got it to-day; and if you carry out your designs, four thousand will have it in the year 1900. We are going to save you from your own folly. We propose to help the people, so that they can have money with which to travel on the railroads, with which to transport their products, and so that your stocks will earn you dividends in spite of yourselves.

We are going to make your stocks in railroad securities, or in every legitimate enterprise, pay you dividends whether you want them or no. Your course is to put them into the hands of receivers. Our course is to put the profits into the hands of the stockholders and into the hands of every man who has put an honest dollar into these enterprises. We have respect for the wishes and the needs and the opportunities and successes of the rich as well as the poor; but we cannot divide and say that one class shall have all and the other class none of the benefits of government.

But, Mr. Speaker, I am told that the Republicans are going to join with the Democrats to repeal this bill. And what Republicans? The Republicans of the East and the Democrats of the East. I tell you, the man who thinks over the situation of this nation to-day is forced to the belief that the salvation of this country, if we are to have a country worth saving, depends upon the men living west of the Delaware River and south of Mason and Dixon's line. [Applause.] You can not longer commit your interests to those whose interests are antagonistic to your own. I find that you gold men agree, and you applaud each other, regardless of your politics; and there comes to my mind a scene that is depicted in Holy Writ, the blackest scene, the most cruel and wicked scene, where truth incarnate was betrayed to the rulers, and which tells us that Pilate, finding no fault in Him, sent Him to Herod; but Herod, not having the power of death, sent Him back to Pilate, demanding His crucifixion; and Pilate delivered Him over to death. And right following that comes this passage:

And the same day Pilate and Herod were made friends together; for before they were at enmity between themselves.

[Laughter.]

Now I can understand how there are no party lines on this question. When you have the people nailed to the cross you can agree to become friends from that day forward. [Laughter.]

My friend from Ohio [Mr. HARTER] told us about the prosperity of England and the prosperity of every nation that had a monometallic standard. He told you how since the stoppage of silver coinage in India prosperity had dawned over the whole nation. Now, I have not got time to answer the gentleman, but I will just read some headings in the New York Sun of yesterday, a good Democratic paper:

RAN RIOT IN BOMBAY—FURY OF RELIGIOUS HATRED BEYOND MILITARY CONTROL—GREAT LOSS OF LIFE AND PROPERTY—EUROPEANS FLOCK TO THE GOVERNMENT BUILDINGS FOR SAFETY.

A Cabinet Consultation in London—Late Dispatches Indicate that the Government Hopes Soon to Check the Turmoil— * * * —A Bombay Merchant's Opinion—The Silver Situation has Created a Great Army of Unemployed in India.

Damoder Gordhundas, a merchant of Bombay, who is staying at the Fifth Avenue Hotel, was greatly interested in the reports of the rioting in that city. "I feel that the reports are exaggerated," said he. "The action of the government in suspending the free coinage of silver has closed the mints and the mills until the army of the unemployed in Bombay numbers in the thousands. This great body of unemployed laborers and mechanics may have taken advantage of the occasion offered by the religious riot to make a serious demonstration."

Now, against the gentleman from Ohio I set the gentleman from India. [Laughter.] But I enjoy hearing the Ohio man talk, for he comes out and says just what he wants. He argues that the less money a nation has, the happier it is, and the more prosperous; and by a parity of reasoning, the less money the gentleman has, the happier he is; but I do not believe that. [Laughter.] I believe that the gentleman uses this expression in a Pickwickian sense.

Why, my friends, just consider that proposition for a moment. If we could draw a line about the city of Washington and erect a wall, do you not suppose if you could take away half of all the money in the city of Washington that the one-half of the money remaining would still buy all the products of industry that are for sale in the city of Washington, just as effectually buy them as the whole would before?

If you could give three hundred men in the city of Washington $100 apiece, and that was all the money there was in this city, all that could get into it, that money would buy every dollar's worth of property in the city of Washington that was for sale. The price goes down to correspond with the volume. That has been the history of the ages.

Let me state some economic axioms: When you double the money of a nation you divide the debt; and if you divide the money you double the debt. Double the money, you double the price; divide the money, you divide the price.

I learned when a boy at school that old mathematical axiom, that when you double sums you double the differences. That twice two is four and the difference between two and four is two, and that twice four is eight, and the difference between four and eight is four. Apply the same reasoning here, and you see that it does not make any difference whether it is little or much, it will just be the same in result. If a man works for a dollar a day and works for thirty days, he will recieve $30; and when be pays $5 a barrel for flour, you will say that if he works for $2 a day he receives $60, and if he pays $10 a barrel for flour he would be no better off. Now if he worked for a dollar a day and paid $5 a barrel for flour he has $25 left; when he has worked thirty days at $2 a day and paid $10 for his barrel of flour he has $50 left, has he not? Now, in which case is he the better off? Especially if he is a debtor. It would not make so much difference if all men were out of debt and paying cash, but there are $32,000,000,000 of indebtedness in the United States, national, State and corporation, municipal and private.

With $3,600,000,000 as the total gold of the whole world, how are we going to pay off this debt? Do you want to double it? You carry out your designs to make silver a mere legal tender for sums of $5. which are your designs, and which you do not hesitate privately to avow—you divide the money, and just as sure as twice two is four you have doubled the debt of every debtor; you have doubled the income of every creditor.

Anglo-American bondholders wish a gold standard because in 1907, only fourteen years hence, some five hundred and fifty millions of bonds now payable by their express terms in coin of standard value will fall due. If we destroy silver as coin of standard value the bond will then by its term become payable in gold. These people well know that the Government will have enough silver and gold in the Treasury to pay these bonds at maturity, but never enough gold, and they wish to force a new mortgage upon the industry of the nation and dictate their own terms concerning such mortgage.

Mr. Speaker, the Republican party, who have for over thirty years had control of the finances of the nation, proudly point to their successful management thereof. They cite the fact that the indebtedness of the nation in 1866 was about $2,800,000,000, and that now the bonded debt of the nation is only $585,000,000. With their boasting they forget to tell you that in principal, interest, and premium on the bonds we have paid about $4,000,000,000, and that it would take about as much of the products of industry to pay the little balance yet remaining as it would to have paid the whole debt in 1866. It would take to-day to pay off the little balance 312,000,000 pounds more of cotton than would have sufficed to pay off the entire debt in cotton in 1866. Year after year production has been paying off interest and principal, and all the time the debt, instead of diminishing, has been increasing.

Let me entreat, gentlemen, to fully consider the consequences that must ensue if you, by unconditional repeal, further lower the price of silver. Consider what plea shall justify you to the producers of wheat, corn, and cotton. What plea will be accepted by the toilers of the nation who see by your votes their debts doubled and the opportunities for a comfortable existence forever swept away? Mr. Speaker, my vote shall be cast before you as it would be cast before the great white throne which has decreed that I am my brother's keeper.

How I like to hear the gentleman from Ohio [Mr. HARTER] bubble over, because he does it in such an easy, pleasant way. He heaves and pitches, and springs a leak here and springs a leak there. [Laughter.] The only thing that I can think of that reminds me of my friend is Mark Twain's description of the storm on the Erie Canal. Speaking of the canal boat in a storm, he says:

She heaved and sot, and sot and heaved,
And high her rudder flung,
And every time she sot and heaved
A mighty leak she sprung.

[Great laughter.]

Mr. Speaker, history has built great monuments upon the plains of the past to mark the point where two roads part. She has erected great light-houses along the shores of Time to warn the passing mariner of the sunken rocks and hidden reefs. Let us observe some of these lights. Moses went down to old Pharaoh, in Egypt, and demanded the deliverance of the people of Israel from the house of bondage, and Pharaoh's answer was the same tale "of brick without straw." Charles the First attempted to coerce Parliament, and he lost his head, and human liberties took a long step forward and upwards. When the people of France cried for bread, a flippant queen asked, "Why they ate not cake." Some day, when a complacent De Brez, knight of the bedchamber, shall enter these Halls and intimate the king's pleasure and our duty, there shall arise some modern Mirabeau, who, driving him hence, will tell him we are here by the will of God and the voice of the sovereign people, to whom alone we owe allegiance and to whose mandates alone we bow.

Our fathers in these colonies pleaded, humbly entreated, of old England to stay the hand of oppression, and asked her to remove the hands of greed which plucked from them the fruits of their toil, and the reply of George III was the imposition of heavier burdens. Our reply was the Declaration of Independence; that wonderful document which embraces the rights of man; if I were to read it in this House I fear it would be a strange message to many. Like the preaching of Paul, "to the Jews a stumbling block, to the Greeks foolishness." [Laughter and applause.] It would be held as a communistic production and its authors demagogues [laughter], because it dared to tell England the truth, and that we were independent and existed without caring either for her crowns or favors.

Why, my friends, to-day all over this land the cry of the people is heard, the banks are failing, not from lack of abundant assets; they have got large surpluses, they even hold great quantities of Government bonds, and yet are forced to suspend. Factories are being closed, mechanics are unemployed, stores are without customers, three millions of idle men are walking up and down asking for an opportunity to earn bread for the hungry ones at home.

Why is this? Is it because of too much money? Is it because of silver money? No; for silver will pay a debt, will buy as much bread, will clothe as many naked as any other dollar. These results come because of the lack of a dollar of any kind; they come from the inability of the people to effect exchanges between one commercial center and another. These New York bankers started their little panic in pursuance of their plan to pinch the West and South and coerce the members of this body into their views. I have read of great masses of rock so nicely poised upon a point that a child could set them in motion, but an army could not stay them after they were once started down the declivity.

So it is with this panic. It is like a conflagration, and we are not here to inquire into the cause of the conflagration. It may be a case of arson [laughter] or it may be a case of "logical evolution," for the gentleman from New York [Mr. HENDRIX] told us that we are "evoluting" toward the gold standard. [Laughter.] I agree with the gentleman that the process of evolution has been going on for twenty years, and it has evoluted the wealth heretofore so evenly distributed among the people of this country into the pockets of the twenty-four thousand. While we have been "evoluting" toward a gold basis we have been "evoluting" toward that condition which confronted all the nations of ancient times just before they lost their liberties. Evolution! It has been said that evolution comes from a full stomach, but there is another thing that comes from an empty stomach, and it is called "revolution." [Laughter and applause.]

I warn you, gentlemen, that the people of to-day are aroused. For years the people have demanded more money, and you meet that demand with a proposition to take away one-half of what they already have! Is that your answer? Can statesmen be so blinded to the interests of the people, the rich and the poor alike, as to carry this design further, in face of the protests of the sixty-seven million toilers of this land?

Oh, Mr. Speaker, in 1776 our forefathers, despite the protests of the Tories of that day, declared their political independence of Great Britain, and so to-day, despite the howling of the "Tories" of this House and their friends in the lobbies, the time has come when by the grace of God we can well declare our financial independence of the same power. [Applause.]

Mr. Speaker, the friends of bimetallism stand here and plead the cause of those who have not easy access to the seat of power, of the men who can not afford to maintain lobbies to throng the corridors of this Capitol building, of the men who can not afford to go to the expensive hotels of this city and sit down to influence the members of this body. But, gentlemen of the other side, you can keep your lobby, if you please, of stock-brokers and gamblers and *Chevalier d'Industrie.* [Laughter.] They can stay here and drink their champagne frappe, eat their canvas-back and terrapin. Very few of those who are back of us are present here, but we have thousands of communications telling us that the people are on their knees in prayer while we are fighting their battles here, and that is more to us than all your packed lobbies.

Mr. Speaker, we have come to the fork of the roads. This means either bimetallism, free-silver coinage with 100 cents in every dollar from this time forth, or it means the utter annihilation of silver as money all over the globe. We have indeed come to the fork of the roads. We have traveled the one road before and we have found it safe. It is no experiment. Along this way our fathers saw the nation grow and expand, and from small beginnings become one of the mightiest of the earth. We have been this way before. Along this road our fathers carried to a successful termination two great foreign wars, and on this road was maintained the mightiest conflict of modern ages, which preserved intact the liberties and the unity of the State. This is no new road. This is such a road as was described by the Psalmist when he said:

Her ways are ways of pleasantness and all her paths are peace.

But there is another road that leads, no man knows where. No human foot upon this continent has ever trod its trackless wilds. I am afraid it is the road that old Solomon spoke of when he said:

There is a way which seemeth right unto a man, but the end thereof are the ways of death.

[Laughter, and applause.]

Mr. Speaker, I think this must be the occasion that the prophet Amos had in mind, looking down through the long vista of the future, when he said:

Hear this, O, ye that swallow up the needy, even to make the poor of the land to fail; * * * making the ephah small and the shekel great, and falsifying the balances by deceit. * * * Shall not the land tremble for this, and every one mourn that dwelleth therein?

Mr. Speaker, that is pretty nearly prophecy. Our land is in mourning and trembling to-day because these men have made the bushel small and the shekel great.

Mr. McCLEARY of Minnesota. Will the gentleman permit a question?

Mr. SIBLEY. Yes, sir.

Mr. McCLEARY of Minnesota. I beg the gentleman's pardon for interrupting at this point, but I could not sooner get the opportunity. The gentleman has been speaking of prophecy. A short time ago he sent a prophecy to the desk to be read; will he please name the gentleman whose prophecy he had read by the Clerk?

Mr. SIBLEY. That was the prophet of the devil. This is the prophet of God Almighty. [Laughter and applause.] That prophet belonged on your side.

Mr. McCLEARY of Minnesota. I did not ask the gentleman to characterize the prophet; I asked him to name him.

Mr. SIBLEY. Ernest Seyd.

Mr. McCLEARY of Minnesota. Is that the same gentleman whom you accuse of having come over here in 1873 as an emissary to "down" silver?

Mr. SIBLEY. I did not utter such accusation. I will append to my remarks what distinguished gentlemen have said—how, sent here as a friend of silver, that man betrayed it—how he came into this House, went with your committees, and showed his dexter hand all through. That will be incorporated in my remarks. I will try to make it plain to the gentleman.

Mr. McCLEARY of Minnesota. My question is, Is this the same gentleman whom you accuse of that "villiany?"

Mr. SIBLEY. No doubt about it, sir.

Mr. McCLEARY of Minnesota. Then I ask that the Clerk read that prophecy again.

Mr. SIBLEY. Everybody has heard it read. If it is the same quotation——

Mr. McCLEARY of Minnesota. The same.

Mr. SIBLEY. Then why have it read twice?

Mr. McCLEARY of Minnesota. If you object to it, then I ask gentlemen to read it in the quiet of their closets, and ask themselves whether the man who used that language could have done the thing you say he did.

Mr. SIBLEY. Yes, sir; I have seen men sell out within the last two months. [Laughter.] From the time he uttered that prophecy two years had elapsed. I have known men to change their minds in twenty minutes. Wise men, it is said, change their minds often; fools, never.

Mr. McCLEARY of Minnesota. What the gentleman says can not be true of a man who died in the cause of silver, as Ernest Seyd did.

Mr. PENCE. When the gentleman speaks of his having "died" does he mean he changed his colors? [Laughter.]

Mr. McCLEARY of Minnesota. The gentleman from Pennsylvania had sufficient regard for Mr. Seyd to quote him as an authority in behalf of silver. Simple justice demands that his memory be treated with fairness. Both before and after 1873 Ernest Seyd was recognized as one of the foremost champions of silver in

Europe, a man whose opinion was eagerly sought by the silver commission of 1876, and of whom Mr. Horton, the bimetallist, said, speaking of Mr. Seyd's death at the international monetary conference of 1881:

It was the profound interest which he took in the conference which brought him here and hastened his death.

This unfounded charge against the memory of a man now unable to defend himself (and I believe that the gentleman from Pennsylvania would not willingly do anyone an injustice) has nothing to do with the merits of this discussion, even if it were true; and I'am glad that the gentleman from Pennsylvania has selected so good a quotation to show the real position of Mr. Seyd.

Mr. SIBLEY. Thank you; in the name of sixty-seven millions of American citizens we plead for more money; and in the name of twenty-four thousand you not only refuse our demand, but purpose the taking away of one-half of what we have left. Prompted alone by our love for rich and poor, by our love for the welfare and peace of our common country, let us warn you that the masses of the people are aroused. All over this fair land they are on their knees in prayer. Their wails have been heard at the throne of the Almighty. My friends, hunger and cold know no philosophy and respect no laws; and when these twin devils are let loose and you force them out upon the world—

Then woe to the robbers who gather
  In fields where they never have sown;
Who have stolen the jewels from labor,
  And builded to Mammon a throne.

For the throne of their god shall be crumbled,
  And the scepter be swept from his hand,
And the heart of the haughty be humbled,
  And a servant be chief in the land.

For the Lord of the harvest hath said it,
  Whose lips never uttered a lie,
And his prophets and poets have read it,
  In symbols of earth and of sky;

That to him who hath reveled in plunder
  'Till the angel of conscience is dumb,
The shock of the earthquake and thunder,
  And tempest and torrent shall come.

[Loud applause.]

The following are the articles and notes to which Mr. SIBLEY referred in his remarks and which he asked to have appended thereto:

Here is what Mr. Hooper, the chairman of the Committee on Coinage, Weights and Measures, and who reported the bill, said in regard to the measure, and of Mr. Ernest Seyd, on the floor of the House.

"The bill was prepared two years ago, and has been submitted to careful and deliberate examination. It has the approval of nearly all the mint experts of the country and the sanction of the Secretary of the Treasury. Ernest Seyd, of London, a distinguished writer and bullionist, is now here, and has given great attention to the subject of mints and coinage, and after examining the first draft of the bill made various sensible suggestions, which the committee accepted and embodied in the bill. While the committee take no credit to themselves for the original preparation of this bill, they have no hesitation in unanimously recommending its passage as necessary and expedient." (See page 2304, *Congressional Globe*, April 9, 1872.)

—

Below will be found a few extracts from different United States Senators and Representatives as they appear in the CONGRESSIONAL RECORD. Let us take the words of Senator ALLISON, of Iowa, first. They are:

"But when the secret history of this bill of 1873 comes to be told it will disclose the fact that the House of Representatives intended to coin both gold and silver, and intended to place both metals upon the French relation instead of our own, which was the true scientific position with reference to this subject in 1873, but that the bill afterwards was doctored, if I may use the term, and I use it in no offensive sense, of course——"

* * * * * * * * * * * *

"I said I used the word in no offensive sense. It was changed after the discussion, and the dollar of 420 grains was substituted for it."—*Congressional Record*, volume 7, part 2, Forty-fifth Congress, second session, page 1063.

"In connection with the charge that I advocated the bill which demonetized the standard silver dollar, I say that, though the chairman of the Committee on Coinage, I was ignorant of the fact that it would demonetize the silver dollar or of its dropping the silver dollar from our system of coins as were those distinguished Senators, Messrs. Blaine and VOORHEES, who were then members of the House, and each of whom, a few days since, interrogated the other: 'Did you know it was dropped when the bill passed?' 'No,' said Mr. Blaine. 'Did you?' 'No,' said Mr. VOORHEES. I do not think that there were three members in the House that knew it. doubt whether Mr. Hooper, who, in my absence from the Committee on Coinage and attendance on the Committee on Ways and Means, managed the bill, knew it. I say this in justice to him."—*Judge Kelley, of Pennsylvania*, in CONGRESSIONAL RECORD, volume 7, part 2, Forty-fifth Congress, second session, page 1605.

Mr. BECK. Will the gentleman from Massachusetts [Senator Dawes] allow me to say a word? The Senator from Massachusetts will recollect that I have not said a word about the history of the demonetization bill, except in a response to questions from the Senator from Iowa [Mr. ALLISON].

* * * * *

Mr. DAWES. The distinguished Englishman, to whom I referred, who was charged with having come over here to do the opposite of what he did, was Ernest Seyd.

Mr. BECK. I observe, if the gentleman will allow me, that on the 9th day of April, 1872, when the bill was read up to its sixth section and laid aside and never taken up again, the gentleman from Massachusetts [Mr. Hooper] remarked:

"The bill was prepared two years ago, and has been submitted to careful and deliberate examinations. It has the approval of nearly all the mint experts of the country, and the sanction of the Secretary of the Treasury. Mr. Ernest Seyd, of London, a distinguished writer who has given great attention to the subject of mints and coinage, after examining the first draft of the bill, furnished many valuable suggestions which have been incorporated in the bill."

"I suppose he is the same person."

Mr. DAWES. There is no doubt about that fact. (See page 125 CONGRESSIONAL RECORD, December 12, 1877.)

Mr. VOORHEES. I want to ask my friend from Maine, whom I am glad to designate in that way, whether I may call him as one more witness to the fact that it was not generally known whether silver was demonetized. Did he know, as the Speaker of the house, presiding at that time, that the silver dollar was demonetized in the bill to which he alludes?

"Mr. BLAINE. I did not know anything that was in the bill at all. As I have said before, little was known or cared on the subject. [Laughter.] And now I should like to exchange questions with the Senator from Indiana, who was then on the floor and whose business, far more than mine, to know, because by the designation of the House I was to put the question; the Senator from Indiana, then on the floor of the House, with his power as a debater, was to unfold them to the House. Did he know?"

"Mr. VOORHEES. I frankly say that I did not."—*Congressional Record*, Feb. 15, 1878, page 1063.

"It passed by fraud in the House, never having been printed in advance, being a substitute for the printed bill; never having been read at the Clerk's desk, the reading having been dispensed with by an impression that the bill made no material alteration in the coinage laws; it was passed without discussion, debate being cut off by operation of the previous question. It was passed, to my certain information, under such circumstances that the fraud escaped the attention of some of the most watchful as well as the ablest statesmen in Congress at the time. * * * Aye, sir, it was a fraud that smells to heaven. It was a fraud that will stink in the nose of posterity, and for which some persons must give account in the day of retribution."—*Mr. Bright, of Tennessee*, in CONGRESSIONAL RECORD, volume 7, part 1, second session Forty-fifth Congress, page 584.

"Why the act of 1873, which forbids the coinage of the silver dollar, was passed no one at this day can give a good reason."—*Senator Bogy, of Missouri*, in CONGRESSIONAL RECORD, volume 4, part 5, Forty-fourth Congress, first session, page 4178.

"It [the bill demonetizing silver] never was understood by either House of Congress. I say that with full knowledge of the facts. No newspaper reporter—and they are the most vigilant men I ever saw in obtaining information—discovered that it had been done."—*Senator Beck, of Kentucky*, in CONGRESSIONAL RECORD, volume 7, part 1, Forty-fifth Congress, second session, page 260.

The Coinage act of 1873, unaccompanied by any written report upon the subject from any committee, and unknown to the members of Congress who, without opposition, allowed it to pass under the belief, if not assurance, that it made no alteration in the value of the current coins, changed the unit of value from silver to gold.—*Mr. Buchard of Illinois*, in CONGRESSIONAL RECORD, July 13, 1876, page 581.

I have before me the record of the proceedings of this House on the passage of that measure, which no man can read without being convinced that the measure and the method of its passage through this House was a "colossal swindle." I assert that the measure never had the sanction of this House, and it does not possess the moral force of law.—*Mr. Holman of Indiana*, in CONGRESSIONAL RECORD, volume 4, part 6, Forty-fourth Congress, first session, Appendix, page 193.

This legislation was had in the Forty-second Congress, February 12, 1873, by a bill to regulate the mints of the United States, and practically abolished silver as money by failing to provide for the coinage of the silver dollar. It was not discussed, as shown by the RECORD, and neither members of Congress nor the people understood the scope of the legislation.—*Joseph Cannon*, in CONGRESSIONAL RECORD, volume 4, part 6, Forty-fourth Congress, first session, Appendix, page 193.

Did the people demonetize silver? Never! It can not even be fairly said that Congress did it. It was done in a corner, darkly. It was done at the instigation of the bondholders and other money kings, who now with upturned eyes deplore the wickedness we exhibit in asking the question even, who did the great wrong against the toiling millions of our people? * * *

How will Congress answer these people except to say that the silver dollar weighing 412½ grains was an honest dollar until the 12th of February, 1873, when we destroyed the money in your pockets and left a vast debt hanging over you, since when our bonds have been sold from hand to hand in the markets among stock gamblers. They knew that we had stricken down your rights and trusted to our honor that your rights should be restored. It would be dishonest in us to restore your money to its value and vitality. It is bullion now—mere pig metal—and is no longer money.—*Senator Morgan*, in CONGRESSIONAL RECORD, December 12, 1877, page 144.

Mr. President. I now come to one of the most remarkable and to my mind one of the most fraudulent pieces of legislation this or any other country ever saw. I refer to the manner of the passage of the bill demonetizing silver. I will not occupy the time of the Senate by going over the whole history of this most iniquitous transaction. Mr. Hooper, since deceased, was at the time chairman of the committee having charge of a bill which had been referred to his committee, and on May 27, 1872, reported a substitute and moved to suspend the rules and pass the substitute, upon which motion, among other things, the following occurred, which any Senator can find by turning to the CONGRESSIONAL GLOBE, part 5, page 3383, and is as follows:

Mr. HOLMAN. I suppose it is intended to have the bill read before it is put on its passage.

The SPEAKER. The substitute will be read.

Mr. HOOPER of Massachusetts, I hope not. It is a long bill, and those who are interested in it are perfectly familiar with its provisions.

Mr KERR. The rules can not be suspended so as to dispense with the reading of the bill.

The SPEAKER. They can be.

Mr. KERR. I want the House to understand that it is attempted to put through this bill without being read.

The SPEAKER. Does the gentleman from Massachusetts [Mr. Hooper] move that the reading of the bill be dispensed with.

Mr. HOOPER of Massachusetts. I will so frame my motion to suspend the rules that it will dispense with the reading of the bill.

The SPEAKER. The gentleman from Massachusetts moves that the rules be suspended and that the bill pass, the reading thereof being dispensed with.

Mr. RANDALL. Can not we have a division of this motion?

The SPEAKER. A motion to suspend the rules can not be divided.

Mr. RANDALL. I should like to have the bill read, although I am willing that the rules shall be suspended as to the passage of the bill.

The question was put on suspending the rules and passing the bill without reading; and (two-thirds not voting in favor thereof) the rules were not suspended.

* * * * * * * * *

Mr. HOOPER of Massachusetts, I now move that the rules be suspended, and the substitute for the bill in relation to mints and coinage passed; and I ask that the substitute be read.

The Clerk began to read the bill.

Mr. BROOKS. Is that the original bill?

The SPEAKER. The motion of the gentleman from Massachusetts [Mr. Hooper] applies to the substitute, and that on which the House is called to act is being read.

Mr. BROOKS. As there is to be no debate, the only chance we have to know what we are doing is to have both the bill and the substitute read.

The SPEAKER. The motion of the gentleman from Massachusetts being to suspend the rules and pass the substitute, it gives no choice between the two bills. The House must either pass the substitute or none.

Mr. BROOKS. How can we choose between the original bill and the substitute unless we hear them both read?

The SPEAKER. The gentleman can vote "ay" or "no" on this question whether this substitute shall be passed.

Mr. BROOKS. I am very much in the habit of voting "no" when I do not know what is going on.

Mr. HOLMAN. Before the question is taken upon suspending the rules and passing the bill, I hope the gentleman from Massachusetts will explain the leading changes made by this bill in the existing law, especially in reference to the coinage. It would seem that all the small coinage of the country is intended to be recoined.

Mr. HOOPER of Massachusetts. This bill makes no changes in the existing law in that regard. It does not require the recoinage of the small coins.

* * * * * * * * *

The question being taken on the motion of Mr. Hooper of Massachusetts to suspend the rules and pass the bill, it was agreed to; there being—ayes 110, noes 13.

And so the rules were suspended, and the substitute passed without its ever being read or any member of that body knowing the contents of it. (See speech of Senator Hereford of West Virginia in CONGRESSIONAL RECORD, December 14, 1877, page 206.)

I know that the bondholders and monopolists of this country are seeking to destroy all the industries of this people in their greed to enhance the value of their gold. I know that the act of 1873 did more than all else to accomplish that result, and the demonetization act of the Revised Statutes was an illegal and unconstitutional consummation of the fraud. I want to restore that money to where it was before, and thus aid in preventing the consummation of their designs.—*Speech by Senator Beck*, of Kentucky, page 258, CONGRESSIONAL RECORD, January 11, 1878.

The silver dollar is peculiarly the laboring man's dollar, as far as he may desire specie. * * * Throughout all the financial panics that have assailed this country, no man has been bold enough to raise his hand to strike it down; no man has ever dared to whisper of a contemplated assault upon it; and when the 12th day of February, 1873, approached, the day of doom to the American dollar, the dollar of our fathers, how silent was the work of the enemy! Not a sound, not a word, no note of warning to the American people that their favorite coin was about to be destroyed as money; that the greatest financial revolution of modern times was in contemplation and about to be accomplished against their highest and dearest rights! The tax-payers of the United States were no more notified or consulted on this momentous measure than the slaves on a Southern plantation before the war, when their master made up his mind to increase their task or to change them from a corn to a cotton field.

Never since the foundation of the Government has a law of such vital and tremendous import, or indeed of any importance at all, crawled into our statute books so furtively and noiselessly as this. Its enactment there was as completely unknown to the people, and indeed to four-fifths of Congress itself, as the presence of a burglar in a house at midnight to its sleeping inmates. This was rendered possible partly because the clandestine movement was so utterly unexpected, and partly from the nature of the bill in which it occurred. The silver dollar of American history was demonetized in an act entitled "An act revising and amending the laws relative to the mints, assay offices, and coinage of the United States." (See speech of Senator VOORHEES in CONGRESSIONAL RECORD, January 15, 1878, page 332.)

I wonder that silver is not already coming into the market to supply the deficiency in the circulating medium. * * * Experience has proved that it takes about $40,000,000 of fractional currency to make the small change necessary for the transaction of the business of the country. Silver will gradually take the place of this currency, and, further, will become the standard of values, which will be hoarded in a small way. I estimate that this will consume from $200,000,000 to $300,000,000 in time of this species of our circulating medium. * * * I confess to a desire to see a limited hoarding of money. But I want to see a hoarding of something that is a standard of value the world over. Silver is this * * *

Our mines are now producing almost unlimited amounts of silver, and it is becoming a question, "What shall we do with it?" I here suggest a solution which will answer for some years to put it in circulation, keeping it there until it is fixed, and then we will find other markets.—*Extract from a letter written by President Grant to Mr. Coudry*, October 13, 1873, eight months after he had signed the bill demonetizing silver, not knowing what that measure contained. See page 208, CONGRESSIONAL RECORD, December 14, 1877.

Horace Greeley saw what but comparatively few saw as clearly as he did, viz., that the establishment of the British system meant slavery not only to the blacks, but to the whites; and these were the words for which the bankers of New York drove him from the office of the Tribune with a broken heart to the grave. He said:

"We boast of having liberated 4,000,000 of slaves. True, we have stricken the shackles from the former bondsmen and brought all laborers to a common level, but not so much by elevating the former slaves as by practically reducing the whole working population to a state of serfdom. While boasting of our noble deeds we are careful to conceal the ugly fact that by our iniquitous monetary system we have nationalized a system of oppression more refined, but none the less cruel than the old system of chattel slavery."

Senator Ingalls said in a speech in this city on February 15, 1878: "No people in a great emergency ever found a faithful ally in gold. It is the most cowardly of all metals. It makes no treaty it does not break. It has no friends it does not sooner or later betray.

"Armies and navies are not maintained by gold. In times of panic and calamity, shipwreck, and disaster, it becomes the agent and minister of ruin. No nation ever fought a great war by the aid of gold. On the contrary, in the crisis of the greatest peril, it becomes the greatest enemy, more potent than the foe in the field; but when the battle is won and peace has been secured, gold reappears and claims the fruits of victory. In our own civil war it is doubtful if the gold of New York and London did not work us greater injury than the powder and lead and iron of the rebels.

"It was the most invincible enemy of the public credit. Gold paid no soldier or sailor. It refused the national obligations. It was worth most when our fortunes were the lowest. Every defeat gave it increased value. It was in open alliance with our enemies the world over, and all its energies were evoked for our destruction.

"But as usual, when danger had been averted and the victory secured, gold swaggers to the front and asserts the supremacy."

CHICAGO PLATFORM.

The following is the full text of the resolutions adopted at Chicago:

"Whereas bimetallism is as ancient as human history; certainly for more than three thousand years gold and silver came down through the ages hand in hand, their relations to each other having varied but a few points in all that vast period of time, and then almost invariably through legislation; and

"Whereas the two metals are named together indissolubly united in the Constitution of the United States as the standard of value of this country, placed there by George Washington, Thomas Jefferson, John Adams, Alexander Hamilton and their associates, and subsequently indorsed and defended by Andrew Jackson and Abraham Lincoln; and

"Whereas silver, one of these ancient metals, was, in the year 1873, without any previous demand by any political party or by any part of the people, or even by any newspapers, and without public discussion, stricken down from the place it had occupied since the days of Abraham and the Pharaohs, under circumstances of such secrecy that Allen G. Thurman, James B. Beck, William M. Stewart, Daniel W. Voorhees, James G. Blaine, then Speaker of the House; James A. Garfield, William D. Kelley, and others present and voting for the bill, as Senators or Representatives, subsequently, repeatedly and publicly declared that they did not know until long afterward that so great and grave a change had been made in the financial system founded by the fathers of the Republic; and

"Whereas the debates in Congress show that the parentage of the measure was in part ascribed by friends of the bill to one Ernest Seyd, a London banker, who, it is claimed, was sent over to Washington by the moneyed classes of the Old World to secure its passage by secret and corrupt means; and

"Whereas President Grant, who signed the bill, declared long subsequently that he did not know that it demonetized silver; and

"Whereas the purpose of this attack upon one of the two ancient precious metals of the world was, by striking down one-half of the money supply, to wit, silver, to double the purchasing power of the remainder, gold, by making it the equivalent of everything possessed or produced by the labor of man, thus reducing the price of all commodities, arresting enterprise, impoverishing the toiler, and degrading mankind; that these results were not only inevitable but forseen appears by the following language used at that time by the then president of the Bank of France, who said: 'If by a stroke of the pen they suppress one of these metals in the monetary service they double the demand for the other metal, to the ruin of all debtors;' and

"Whereas the awful consequences thus prophesied are now upon the people of the whole world, we stand in the midst of unparalleled distress and in the shadow of impending calamities which are beyond estimate. The ruling industry of the people who inhabit one third of the area of this republic has been stricken down, property values destroyed, and the workmen compelled to fly as from pestilence. Everywhere over this broad land the honest toilers, numbering hundreds of thousands, have been thrown out of employment and will have to eat the bitter bread of charity or starve. The products of industry, of the farm and the workshop have depreciated in price, as shown by official and public statistics, until production ceases to be profitable; the money in the country, inadequate for the business of the land, has gravitated to the banks; while the people, distrusting the banks, have demanded their deposits to hoard or hide them: mercantile houses are going to the wall by thousands, because the masses have not the means to buy even the necessities of life; to supply the lack of currency, the banks of the great cities have issued a substitute for money, unknown to the laws, called clearing-house certificates: the movement of the great crops now being gathered demands a vast amount of currency, which the banks are unable to furnish; and in the midst of these conditions the daily press is clamoring for the repeal of the act of July 14, 1890, called the Sherman act, although the repeal of that act means the stoppage of the issue of more than $3,000,000 every month; thus shutting off of the supply of funds for the business of the country in the midst of the terrible conditions which surround us, and ignoring the fact that to hold the balance level between the debtor and creditor classes the supply of currency must increase side by side with the increase of population and business, and that in this nation the growth of population is at the rate of about 37 per cent every ten years, while the increase of business is much greater; and

"Whereas the great expounder of the Constitution, Daniel Webster, said: 'Gold and silver, at rates fixed by Congress, constitute the legal standard of value in this country, and neither Congress nor any State has authority to establish any other standard or to displace that standard;' and

"Whereas the Hon. James G. Blaine, quoting this utterance, adds: 'On the much-vexed and long-mooted question as to a bimetallic or monometallic standard my own views are sufficiently indicated in the remarks I have made. I believe the struggle now going on in this country and in the other countries for a single gold standard would, if successful, produce widespread disaster in and throughout the commercial world. The destruction of silver as money and establishing gold as the sole unit of value must have a ruinous effect on all forms of property except those investments which yield a fixed return in money. These would be enormously enhanced in value and would gain a disproportionate and unfair advantage over every other species of property. If, as the most reliable statistics affirm, there are nearly $7,000,000,000 of coin or bullion in the world, very equally divided between gold and silver, it is impossible to strike silver out of existence as money without results which will prove distressing to millions and utterly disastrous to tens of thousands.'

"Again he said: 'I believe gold and silver coin to be the money of the Constitution; indeed the money of the American people, anterior to the Constitution, which the great organic law recognized as quite independent of its own existence. No power was conferred on Congress to declare either metal should not be money. Congress has, therefore, in my judgment, no power to demonetize both. If, therefore, silver has been demonetized, I am in favor of remonetizing it. If its coinage has been prohibited, I am in favor of ordering it to be resumed. I am in favor of having it enlarged;' and

"Whereas the present Secretary of the Treasury, the Hon. John G. Carlisle, on the floor of the House of Representatives, February 21, 1878, said: 'I know that the world's stock of the precious metals is none too large, and I see no reason to apprehend that it will ever become so. Mankind will be fortunate, indeed, if the annual production of gold and silver coin shall keep pace with the annual increase of population, commerce, and industry. According to my views of the subject, the conspiracy which seems to have been formed here and in Europe to destroy, by legislation and otherwise, from three-sevenths to one-half of the metallic money of the world is the most gigantic crime of this or any other age. The consummation of such a scheme would ultimately entail more misery upon the human race than all the wars, pestilences, and famines that ever occurred in the history of the world. The absolute and instantaneous destruction of half the entire movable property of the world, including houses, ships, railroads, and all other appliances for carrying on commerce, while it would be felt more sensibly at the moment, would not produce anything like the prolonged distress and disorganization of society that must inevitably result from the permanent annihilation of the metallic money in the world;' and

"Whereas Senator John Sherman of Ohio, who more than any other man is responsible for the demonetization of silver, clearly understood the evil consequences of shrinking currenc below the legitimate demand of the business of the country, as evidenced by what he said in the Senate in 1869, to wit: 'The contraction of the currency is a far more distressing operation than Senators suppose. Our own and other nations have gone through that operation before. It is not possible to take that voyage without the sorest distress. To every person except a capitalist out of debt, or a salaried officer or annuitant, it is a period of loss, danger, lassitude of trade, fall of wages, suspension of enterprise, bankruptcy, and disaster. It means ruin to all dealers whose debts are one-half their business capital, though one-third less than their actual property. It means the fall of all agricultural production without any great reduction of taxes. What prudent man would dare to build a house, a railroad, a factory, or a barn with this certain fact before him?'

"Therefore, in view of all these facts, we declare:

"1. That there must be no compromise of this question. All legislation demonetizing silver and restricting the coinage thereof must be immediately and completely repealed by an act restoring the coinage of the country to the conditions established by the founders of the nation and which continued for over eighty years without complaint from any part of our people. Every hour's delay in undoing the corrupt work of Ernest Seyd and our foreign enemies is an insult to the dignity of the American people, a crushing burden on their prosperity, and an attempt to place us again under the yoke from which George Washington and his compatriots rescued us.

"We protest against the financial policy of the United States being made dependent upon the opinion or policies of any foreign government, and assert the power of this nation to stand on its own feet and legislate for itself upon all subjects.

"2. We declare that the only remedy for our metallic financial troubles is to open the mints of the nation to gold and silver on equal terms, at the old ratio of 16 of silver to 1 of gold. Whenever silver bullion can be exchanged at the mints of the United States for legal-tender silver dollars, worth 100 cents each, that moment 412½ grains of standard silver will be worth 100 cents, and as commerce equalizes the prices of all commodities throughout the world, whenever 412½ grains of standard silver are worth 100 cents in the United States they will be worth that sum everywhere else, and can not be bought for less. While it will be urged that such a result would enhance the price of silver bullion, it is sufficient for us to know that a similar increase would be immediately made in the price of every form of property, except gold and credits, in the civilized world. It would be a shallow selfishness that would deny prosperity to the mining industries at the cost of bankruptcy to the whole people. The legislation to demonetize silver has given an unjust increase to the value of gold at the cost of the prosperity of mankind. Wheat and all other agricultural products have fallen side by side with silver.

"3. That while the 'Sherman act' of July 14, 1890, was a device of the enemy to prevent the restoration of free coinage, and is greatly objectionable because it continues the practical exclusion of silver from the mints and reduces it from a money metal to a commercial commodity, nevertheless its repeal without the restoration of free coinage would stop the expansion of our currency required by our growth in population and business, widen still further the difference between the two precious metals, thus making the return to bimetallism more difficult, greatly increase the purchasing power of gold, still further break down the price of the products of the farmer, the laborer, the mechanic, and the tradesman, and plunge still further all commerce, business, and industry into such depths of wretchedness as to endanger peace, order, the preservation of free institutions, and the very maintenance of civilization. We, therefore, in the name of the Republic and of humanity, protest against the repeal of the said act of July 14, 1890, except by an act restoring free bimetallic coinage, as it existed prior to 1873. We suggest that the maintenance of bimetallism by the United States at the ratio of 16 to 1 will increase our commerce with all the silver-using countries of the world, containing two-thirds of the population of the world, without decreasing our commerce with those nations which buy our raw material, and will compel the adoption of bimetallism by the nations of Europe sooner than by any other means.

"4. We assert that the unparalleled calamities which now afflict the American people are not due to the so-called Sherman act of 1890; and in proof thereof we call attention to the fact that the same evil conditions now prevail over all the gold standard nations of the world. We are convinced that, bad as is the state of affairs in this country, it would have been still worse but for the Sherman act, by which the nation has obtained to some extent an expanding circulation to meet the demands of a continent in process of colonization, and the business exigencies of the most energetic and industrious race that has ever dwelt on the earth, and we insist upon the execution of the law without evasion so long as it is upon the statute books and upon the purchase each month of the full amount of silver that it provides for, to the end that the monthly addition to the circulating medium the law secures shall be maintained

"5. That we would call the attention of the people to the fact that in the midst of all the troubles of the time, the value of the national bonds and the national legal-tender money, whether made of gold, silver, or paper, has not fallen a particle. The distrust is not of the Government or its money, but of the banks which have, as we believe, precipitated the present panic on the country in an ill-advised effort to control the action of Congress on the silver question and the issue of bonds. We invite the bankers to attend to their legitimate business and permit the rest of the people to have their full share in the control of the Government. In this way, they will much sooner restore that confidence which is so necessary to the prosperity of the people. It must not be forgotten that, while boards of trade, chambers of commerce, bankers, and money-dealers are worthy and valuable men in their places, the Republic can more safely repose upon the great mass of its peaceful toilers and producers, and that this 'business man's age' is rapidly exterminating the business men of this country. The time has come when the politics of the nation should revert as far as possible to the simple and pure condition out of which the Republic arose.

"6. We suggest for the consideration of our fellow-citizens that the refusal of the opponents of bimetallism to propose any substitute for the present law or to elaborate any plan for the future, indicate either an ignorance of our financial needs or an unwillingness to take the public into their confidence, and we denounce the attempt to unconditionally repeal the Sherman law as an attempt to secure gold monometallism in flagrant violation of the last national platform of all the political parties.'

www.ingramcontent.com/pod-product-compliance
Lightning Source LLC
Chambersburg PA
CBHW021621290326
41931CB00047B/1388
9783337422684